A Sure Foundation

Volume 21

CHARLES A. COATES
1862 - 1945

Scripture references are generally from the King James Bibles unless otherwise noted.

* * * * *

Page numbering does not correspond to the published index of C.A.C.'s ministry. This is because larger type and page sizes affect the pagination.

This edition is published by:

BIBLES, etc.
www.bibles-etc.com

Layout by: W.S.Chellberg

ISBN: 978-0-912868-30-1

Available from:

www.LuLu.com

Biography of Charles Andrew Coates

This book is part of a large series from original sources of published ministry given over many years by Charles A Coates, who was born in Bradford, England, in December 1862, and died in Teignmouth, Devon in October 1945.

He relates that he started writing and publishing tracts at the age of 22, and by 1900, books collecting his lectures and writings began a limited private circulation. Interest led to more general publication of several collections included in this series. His ministry is now widely appreciated and has been frequently republished. Mr Coates may be best known for a series of Outlines of many books of the Bible. These are later than the collected tracts and lectures, being based on notes of Bible readings from 1920 up until shortly before his death, almost all of which were revised by him. A lot more of his ministry has been published since his death.

Mr Coates' ministry reflects his long life of devoted service to the Lord, and the depth and extent of his love and appreciation of divine truth. It is valued for its clarity and accessibility, and many have been drawn into the study of the Word by starting with one or other of his books. He cuts in a straight line the word of truth; not only accurate in his interpretation, but also direct and faithful in the application of the truth to our walk and conduct. He is sound on the foundations of the gospel, giving extensive guidance and assurance to souls seeking establishment in their faith.

Walter Brown sums up Mr Coates in this introduction to his published letters -

> Our brother's active service was for many years much restricted through bodily weakness, and this contributed, under the Lord's hand, to the development of ... choice spiritual feelings. His mind was remarkably formed by the teaching of the Holy Scriptures, and all that he wrote was the result of prayerful consideration. Hence the combination of unswerving faithfulness to the Lord with true humility and gracious sympathy in the spiritual experiences of others. Above all else, the reader cannot fail to remark in these pages our beloved brother's deep appreciation of the Person of Christ, and his wholehearted devotedness to His interests on earth, centring in "His body, which is the assembly". No matter affecting the Lord or His saints was regarded as too trivial for his interest and prayers, and the smallest service done for His Name and glory found recognition and appreciation.

Charles Coates was born and brought up in Yorkshire. His father, James Coates, was born in Scotland in 1809. James is said to have once been a shepherd, but from no later than 1841, he was a linen draper in Bradford. He was moved to withdraw from the Congregational Chapel there in 1846 to be among the brethren in the town; and in 1855 was married to Elizabeth Rollinson, born in nearby Otley in 1820.

Charles was converted at the age of 16 – a turning point he marked by writing the first of several hymns. Sometime before his mother died in 1905, he moved with her to Paignton, Devon. After she died, he had lodgings in Teignmouth, and lived and broke bread there until his death. He never married. Mr Coates started working with his father as a draper, but evidently gave this up -perhaps when his father died: his health was poor from an early age. His infirmity also limited how much he travelled, so that much of his ministry was either given locally, or written.

This set of books is published with the desire that others may find and get the benefit of what the Lord gave His people through our brother; and that this will be to God's glory.

D. Andrew Burr
January 2021

CONTENTS

A SURE FOUNDATION

To secure *a sure foundation* it is often needful to clear away a lot of rubbish. The wise builder digs "deep"; he removes all that is untrustworthy before he lays a single stone. This is exactly what I desire to do, and I entreat my reader to give earnest consideration to the weighty matters which I shall bring before him. There can be no solid peace until the whole truth of our lost condition as children of Adam is known and accepted. Peace founded upon ignorance and self-deception is common enough; but it is a slumber from which there will be a terrible awakening in eternity, if never before.

It is evident that on such a subject human opinions are perfectly worthless. As to our souls' relations with God, we dare not allow the opinions of men to weigh with us for a single moment. Philosophers may speculate, theologians may reason and dispute, and rationalists may assert the sufficiency of the human mind to pronounce on these solemn questions, but we regard them all with equal distrust. We would as soon think of leaning on a straw, or of crossing Niagara on a spider's web, as of placing any reliance on our own abilities or mental powers in this matter. The Holy Scriptures must be our only authority and guide. We find there unerring truth which carries its own credentials with it, for it searches and exposes us as none but God could, and by so doing proves its divine origin more completely than all the volumes of "Evidences" that were ever written.

Let us then ponder well, and weigh as in the very presence of God, the following grave and momentous statements of Holy Scripture:

"We have before proved both Jews and Gentiles, that they are *all under sin*; as it is written, There is none righteous, no, not one: there is none that understandeth, there is none that seeketh after God. They are all gone out of the way, they are together become unprofitable; there is none that doeth good, no, not one" (Romans 3:9-12).

"That every mouth may be stopped, and all the world may become *subject to the judgment of God*" (Romans3:19; margin).

"By the deeds of the law there shall no flesh be justified in his sight: for by the law is the knowledge of sin" (Romans 3:20).

"*There is no difference: for all have sinned*, and come short of the glory of God" (Romans 3:23).

These are sweeping and comprehensive statements. They are too plain to be misunderstood, and it is impossible for any sober-minded person to regard them with levity or indifference. They do not assert that all Adam's children are alike as to *sinful actions*; but they do proclaim that all are alike "under sin", "subject to the judgment of God", and "come short of the glory of God". Sin displays itself in a thousand different forms in a thousand different individuals. It stalks unblushingly abroad at noonday in the open and profligate sinner. It makes itself obnoxious to men when it violently trespasses upon their interests or pleasures in the form of dishonesty or personal injury, or when it excessively outrages natural and moral decency. But the root-principle from which every sinful action proceeds is the same in every man, woman, and child of Adam's race. It would be difficult to find two lives that were exactly alike outwardly; but when we look beneath the surface, and consider man's *state before God*, we find "there is no difference". The amiable young lady and the industrious man of business are doing their own will and seeking their own pleasure. The drunkard and the thief are doing the same thing on a rather lower platform. It is true that in the one case there may be a certain outward acknowledgment of God which is not found in the other; but this is only a "form of godliness" assumed in order to maintain a good character before men, or to soothe and satisfy a conscience which might otherwise become uncomfortably active.

Instruction as to what is right and wrong is of no avail as a remedy. It has been tried. God has made known to man in the law what he ought to do, and what he ought not to do. Its only effect is to bring home to every awakened conscience "the knowledge of sin". I have no doubt the reader would admit that he had often done things he knew to be contrary to the mind of God. Does not this *prove* that there is something fearfully wrong?

"But if I do my best to please God, and to do what is right, is not that enough?" Well, perhaps you have honestly tried to do this. How have you succeeded? You have promised, resolved, vowed; you have cultivated yourself very carefully, you have read the Bible, and you have prayed earnestly. You have done your best. Now I ask a plain question. Are you satisfied with the result of your efforts? Have you not found out that you are "under sin"? And being "under sin", you must be "subject to the judgment of God".

Additions or subtractions are of no use in such a case. You have tried to get rid of bad habits and to acquire good ones; but the weeds grow faster than you can pluck them up, and the flowers you fain would cultivate wither before they come to perfection. You are slowly beginning to realise that the soil is bad - that no half measures will do - that you have not only done many wrong things, but that you are *all wrong yourself.* What is the use of adding religion or morality to a man who still remains "subject to the judgment of God"?

You may be sure of this, that if you build upon

yourself in any way your labour is vain. Sooner or later the complete worthlessness and instability of such a foundation must be apparent. Many will discover this when eternal ruin has come upon them. They have built without removing the rubbish. They may bear an excellent name among men; they may acquire a great reputation for their sterling moral character; they may hold high positions in religious circles; but they have reared this imposing structure on a heap of rubbish. For in spite of all this they remain "under sin", and they "come short of the glory of God". And if in this state when their day of grace is over they must perish eternally. May God in His mercy preserve you from building upon the rubbish of fallen and sinful flesh.

THE FOUNDATION

The first thing that an awakened sinner feels is that God must be righteous in all His ways. If grace is to reign it must be "through righteousness". Any supposed blessing which does not rest upon a secure basis of righteousness is absolutely worthless. Hence the sure foundation of all blessing is that wondrous act in which the righteousness of God is declared - the death of Christ.

"Whom God hath set forth a propitiation [or mercy-seat] *through faith in his blood*, to declare his righteousness for the remission of sins that are past, through the forbearance of God; to declare, I say, at this time, his righteousness: that he might be just, and the justifier of him which believeth in Jesus" (Romans 3:25-26).

The extreme penalty has passed upon all alike. "The wages of sin is death". "And so death passed upon all men, for that all have sinned" (Romans 3:23; Romans 5:12) The righteousness of God must be against sin, but in the death of Christ we see that righteousness declared in such a way that it becomes the foundation of blessing. God has expressed His judgment of sin in the fullest way without touching a hair of the sinner's head. Nothing could show God's hatred of sin so much as the fact that Christ has died to bear its judgment, while the fact that He has died has silenced the devil as to God's actings in grace. The one who was chief of sinners may go into glory on the ground of that death, forgiveness of sins may be proclaimed to the guilty and perishing millions of Adam's race, and not even Satan can say that God is *unrighteous* in His ways of grace.

I can see God's way of dealing with sin in the death of Christ; I see all that is due to God in respect of sin maintained in that death; in a word, I see His righteousness there. But it is all in my favour. I can fall in with God's righteousness - with God's way of dealing with sin - and find that it secures my blessing for ever. On the ground of the death of Christ, God is as righteous in justifying the ungodly sinner who believes in Jesus as He will be righteous in condemning everyone who has not "faith in His blood". You must learn God's righteousness either in grace or in judgment. The believer learns it in the death of Christ; the unbeliever will learn it in the awful light of the great white throne. Apart from "the precious blood of Christ", the whole weight of God's righteousness must be against you. Thank God! that precious blood is available for you; you may by faith come under its cleansing efficacy and sheltering power; and then "the righteousness of God which is by faith of Jesus Christ" will be upon you, making your blessing eternally sure.

It is of vast importance for us to see that the judgment due to us has not been in any wise mitigated. God's righteousness could only act in one way toward us as children of Adam. We were under His judgment - under the sentence of death. But what was due to us has come upon One who in perfect divine love was found in the place of sin and death. A divine Person has been in this world, *and has died.* So that the righteousness of God is seen in a way that presents it in the strongest possible light. If it were possible for the son of a judge to take the place of a criminal, and the judge passed the full sentence upon him, his righteousness would be more vividly expressed than if he had sentenced the culprit himself. You may depend upon it that no criminal would venture to trifle with such a judge. But God has been so glorified in the death of Christ that His righteousness is "unto all". That is, it is presented in the gospel to every creature under heaven as the only way and ground of blessing for sinners. God has approached man in this wonderful way. He has provided for His own glory, and laid a sure foundation for the blessing of man. Do you fear God? Do you bow in recognition of the solemn fact that you are subject to His judgment, and that the sentence of death has passed upon you? Then you are entitled by faith and through God's grace to put yourself under the - shelter of the precious blood of Christ. You are entitled to take your stand upon the fact that the judgment has been borne, and the sentence righteously executed, to take advantage of God's righteousness, and to fall in with His way of dealing with sin, and if you do so your blessing is certain. God is "the justifier of him which believeth in Jesus".

“WHAT MEANEST THOU?”

It has been estimated that over seventy-five per cent of the inhabitants of this country have no concern about the salvation of their souls. They are not atheists or infidels, nor do they make any profession of being saved; they are simply indifferent to the whole matter. If the thought of having to do with God comes into their minds, they solace themselves by a comparison of their own state with that of their fellows, and they conclude that as they are not worse than others, and perhaps better than many, there is no reason why they should have any concern as to their spiritual state. Any occasional alarm is speedily stilled by the thought that God is merciful - a sentiment which in the mind of an indifferent sinner means that he likes to think of God as One whose judgment of sin is not much more severe than his own. It is to this large body of people, and to each individual in it, that the following plain words are addressed.

You are not indifferent to things which affect your health, your circumstances, the prosperity of your business, or your future in life. Nor are you uninterested in current events and great social movements. You are in deep concern when your child is sick and lies on the borderline between life and death. You spend hours in thought about the interests of your political party. You have regard to the maintenance of your credit, character, and reputation. Then why so indifferent to that which is of vastly greater importance than all these things put together - your eternal salvation? A friendly voice asks you the question which stands at the head of this paper - a question which once rang on the startled ear of Jonah - "What meanest thou, O sleeper?"

You would be the first to condemn the folly of indifference if you saw it displayed when good opportunities presented themselves for pecuniary gain, mental improvement, or social elevation. Yet eternal gain is within your reach, and the greatest possible elevation is offered to you without awakening in your heart the least desire to secure it for yourself. What should we say of a sick man who took no interest in what is known to be an unfailing remedy for his disease? of a culprit sentenced to death who was heedless when tidings of a royal pardon were brought to his cell? of a drowning man who would not regard the life-line which he sees within his reach? you would say of such persons that they were bereft of their senses. Then what must we think of a sinful creature who has no care or anxiety about his soul, and who looks upon the gospel as unworthy of his notice? Surely such indifference is not wise?

But, further than this, it is fraught with danger. To walk blindfold on the edge of a precipice is a dangerous as well as a foolish performance. *Unbelief* does not annihilate God, responsibility, sins, judgment, eternity. The peril is great and real; do not trifle with it. You may remember reading how the signalman at the end of the Tay Bridge crept along the structure on that wild December night amid the fury of the storm, until, peering through the darkness, he could discover the awful chasm through which the tempest was sweeping. You may depend upon it he did not return to his cabin to put the signals right for another train to pass on to the bridge. But what would you have thought of the driver and guard of the next train if, in utter disregard of the signals and of the entreaties of the signalman, they had persisted in going forward, the driver saying, "I don't believe the bridge is down", and the guard adding, "Nobody can know until they get there, and we must take our chance"? You would have exclaimed, "Madmen!" You would have said that they were rushing headlong not only into danger, but into *certain destruction.*

Beware! The signals of Holy Scripture are all against you, and another warning reaches you now as you speed along to eternity. "When they shall say, Peace and safety; then sudden destruction cometh upon them ... and *they shall not escape*" (1 Thessalonians 5:3).

In the year of the Great Plague 90,000 persons died in London. With the earliest symptoms of the disease all indifference fled. Many went mad with terror, and ran screaming through the grass-grown deserted streets, as if to escape from the pursuit of death. Have you no symptoms that might justly fill your conscience with alarm? "The thought of foolishness is *sin*". "To him that knoweth to do good, and doeth it not, to him it is *sin*". "God shall judge *the secrets* of men". The plague of sin is in your heart; your members are yielded as instruments of unrighteousness unto sin; and the end of these things is death. Have you never been astounded at the evil thoughts of your own heart? or are you so thoroughly accustomed to them as to be "abominable and filthy", and to drink "iniquity like water"? (Job 15:16). In any case it is high time for indifference to be thrown off as a dangerous and deadly thing.

Another fact deserves consideration; indifference will *soon have an end.* You may look upon the things of a future life as being a "great secret", and may throw aside all serious thought about them with the flippant assertion that "nobody has come back to tell us". You may treat the soul's relations with God, and all that He has made known, as merely matters of opinion. But such thoughts can only delude you for a very short time. The poor comfort which they yield will be snatched away by the hand of death. The man who probably never prayed on earth prays earnestly in hell (Luke 16). He who would have laughed at any spiritual concern is now anxious about the souls of his brethren. The virgins who cared nothing about the oil until it was too late to buy, were in great diligence about it then, but could only give vent to their anguish in the unanswered cry, "Lord, Lord, open to us". Sad, sad, that bitter wail - "The harvest is past, the summer is ended, and we are not saved".

I would have you to consider carefully that *indifference* to the gospel is a sin of no ordinary kind; it is pure and simple wickedness. To rightly estimate this we must call to mind *what* it is that men treat with indifference. It is the claims *of God* that are set at naught, and the grace *of God* that is despised. The gift of the Son of God, His work of infinite love at Calvary, the glory which that work has thrown open, and all the present blessings of the Salvation of God, are so many *trifles* to the indifferent sinner; he can afford to treat them all with contemptuous disregard, if not disdain. After all the resources of divine love have been taxed to the utmost; after the heart of God has told itself out in the most wonderful way; after all the treasures of heavenly grace have been presented for acceptance, after the invitation has gone forth in its fulness - "Come, for all things are now ready" - the insulting answer which goes back to the giver of the feast is, "I pray thee have me excused; I have other and more important matters in hand; I cannot come".

How you must hate God, when you will perish rather than have His blessings! the hardihood which ventures to brave His wrath is only equalled by the hatred that refuses His grace, and both combine in the indifferent soul. In saying this I am assuming that you have heard the proclamation of grace; but perhaps, in doing so, I am taking too much for granted. Perhaps my reader is entirely ignorant of the good things which God has provided, and which, through His grace, a large number of people in this world are enjoying. Let me say, then, very briefly, that through a crucified, risen, and glorified Saviour - the Son of God, Jesus Christ our Lord - God is proclaiming the forgiveness of sins, and eternal salvation. The *poor* may freely take these priceless blessings, for they are the *gift* of God. The *rich* surely cannot afford to be without them. That they are expressly for the *guilty* and the *lost* is made certain by the very nature of the things in themselves. And as for the *good* and *righteous*, even they may be saved if they cast their pride to the winds, and take the sinner's place in repentance before God.

"God now commandeth all men everywhere to repent" (Acts 17:30).

"God ... will have all men to be saved" (1 Timothy 2:4). It is at an infinite cost that God has secured for Himself in righteousness the title of Saviour God. The Son has been given; Jesus has died; and the whole universe can see at the cross of Christ that God is neither indifferent to sin, nor to the need of His poor creature who has fallen under its power. Then let indifference be banished from your heart. Turn in true repentance to God, and receive by faith the Lord Jesus Christ as your Saviour. For your life hangs on a thread; the record of your sins is on high; and the blackest midnight is brighter than the darkness of a Christless grave. “If thou shalt confess with thy mouth the Lord Jesus, and shalt believe in thine heart that God hath raised him from the dead, thou shalt be saved” (Romans 10:9).

A PREACHER OF THE OLD SCHOOL

Many preachers are giving up the old ideas about the fall and total depravity of man. People are not often plainly told now that they are guilty sinners before a holy God. The sermons of our forefathers - who used to press this so constantly upon their hearers - are looked upon in many quarters as relics of the Dark Ages, only fit for the old curiosity shop. There is, however, one preacher left of the old school, and he speaks today as loudly and as clearly as ever. He is not a popular preacher, though the world is his parish, and he travels over every part of the globe, and speaks in every language under the sun. He visits the poor; he calls upon the rich; you may meet him in the workhouse, or find him moving in the very highest circles of society. He preaches to both Churchmen and Dissenters, to people of every religion and of no religion, and, whatever text he may have, the substance of his sermon is always the same. He is an eloquent preacher; he often stirs feelings which no other preacher could reach, and brings tears into eyes that are little used to weep. He addresses himself to the intellect, the conscience, and the heart of his hearers. His arguments none have been able to refute: there is no conscience on earth that has not at some time quailed in his presence: nor is there any heart that has remained wholly unmoved by the force of his weighty appeals. Most people hate him, but in one way or another he makes everybody hear him.

He is neither refined nor polite. Indeed he often interrupts the public arrangements, and breaks in rudely upon the private enjoyments of life. He lurks about the doors of the theatre and the ball-room; his shadow falls sometimes on the card-table; he is often in the neighbourhood of the public-house; he frequents the shop, the office, and the mill; he has a master-key which gives him access to the most secluded chamber; he appears in the midst of legislators and of fashionable religious assemblies; neither the villa, the mansion, nor the palace daunt him by their greatness; and no court or alley is mean enough to escape his notice. His name is *Death.*

You have heard many sermons from the old preacher. You cannot take up a newspaper without finding that he has a corner in it. Every tombstone serves him for a pulpit. You often see his congregations passing to and from the graveyard. Every scrap of mourning is a memento of one of his visits. Nay, he has often addressed himself to you personally. The sudden departure of that neighbour, the solemn parting with that dear parent, the loss of that valued friend, the awful gap that was left in your heart when that fondly-loved wife, that idolised child, was taken, have all been loud and solemn appeals from the old preacher. Some day very soon he may have you for his text, and in your bereaved family circle and by your graveside he may be preaching to others. Let your heart turn to God this moment to thank Him that you are still in the land of the living - that you have not ere now *died in your sins*!

You may get rid of the Bible; you may disprove - to your own satisfaction - its histories; you may ridicule its teachings: you may despise its warnings; you may reject the Saviour of whom it speaks.

You can get away from the preachers of the gospel, you are not compelled to go to either church, chapel, or mission room; and you can cross over to the other side of the street if there is an open-air meeting. It is in your power to burn this book and every other that comes into your possession. Yea! the time may come when infidelity and priestcraft will combine to make the preaching of Christ by lip or pen a criminal offence.

But if you get rid of God's Word and of God's servants, what will you do with the old preacher of whom I have spoken? Have you some plan to superannuate him - to put him on the retired list? Will you compel him by force to suspend his itinerations? Or do you hope that a few more years of scientific culture and modern thought will have such an effect upon him that his doctrines and practice will be quite changed? It is true that most preachers are more or less affected by the spirit and opinions of the age they live in, but *this* old preacher has gone on in perfect indifference to the changing events and opinions of the whole world for nearly six thousand years. All histories - both sacred and profane - give the same account of him, and all experience confirms it, so that it is against reason to expect that he will change in his old age.

Dying men and women! consider the prospect that is before you. Your little day will soon be passed; your pleasures will have an end; your occupations will be laid aside; your wealth and honours will be worthless to you in the solemn hour when your body is reduced to a few handfuls of dust. After all, you "*must needs die*".

Consider this matter, I pray you. Must there not be a cause for this? Is it by mere accident that a creature with such powers and capacities should come to so ignominious an end? There is but one answer to these questions, and as long as the old preacher goes on his rounds he will continue to proclaim it. Listen! "By one man *sin entered* into the world, and *death by sin*".

Yes! the conclusion is forced upon us - there must be something wrong. We cannot think of fourteen hundred millions of graves being dug every thirty years on this planet of ours, as one whole generation after another passes down to the gates of death, without having the thought that there is something fearfully wrong.

THE FALL OF MAN

is no mere theological dogma, but a fearful reality of which the world's history and the stern sad facts of our own experience bear terrible witness. *Sin* is not simply an ugly word in the Bible or on preachers' lips; it is a dark, foul reality which blights and curses the world by its presence. Nor is there any exception to the scope of its ravages. "Death passed upon *all men*, for that all *have sinned*". My reader is implicated in this matter. There is a great difference between the careless spectator in a court of justice and the criminal in the dock whose life is at stake. The latter is your position. You have sinned: upon you the sentence of death has passed: and very soon it will be said of you as it was said of eight old men in Genesis - "*he died*".

When will you die? Do not think this a foolish question. You count your money; you reckon your profits; you calculate your dividends; surely it is quite as important to number your days! How will you find out? Turn up the life assurance tables. Yes, that is the average. A person of your age has the probability of living so many years. But let us consider a moment. That is an average, is it not? Which means that some live longer and others a good many years shorter. Some have died - very suddenly, too - just about your age. It is possible, is it not, that you may die very soon? A young man went to a divinity professor and asked him how long before death a man ought to be prepared for it. The reply was, "About five minutes". The young man turned away with relief, making up his mind to see life, sow his wild oats, enjoy the pleasures of the world, and then turn to God at the end of his days. "Stop", said the professor; "*When* are you going to die?" "I cannot tell", replied the young man. "Then you had better be prepared for death *now*; you may not have five minutes to live".

How will you die? The first Napoleon, when life was passing away, insisted that his boots should be put on. He would die, like a soldier, in his boots. A great ecclesiastical dignitary died in the splendid robes of his religious office. Queen Elizabeth died crying, "Millions of money for a moment of time". How will you die?

Sad, sad, indeed, if that Word comes true of you which was thrice repeated to some very respectable people a long time ago - "*Ye shall die in your sins*". One second after your death it will be a matter of no consequence to you whether you died in a palace or in a cellar. Little will you care whether you have a national funeral in Westminster Abbey, or your poor body is tossed by unceremonious hands into a pauper's grave. But your whole eternity will hang upon the state in which you die. If sin works such havoc, and sins have such fearful consequences in this world, what must they entail in the next? Men reap as they sow in this world, but God does not definitely execute judgment upon sins in this life. "*After death the judgment*". In this world you can, in a sense, avoid God. Many live "without God in the world". But death dissolves all connection with the things of time by which God can be excluded, and beyond death you must *have to do with God.*

A notable infidel, when dying, said, "I would give £30,000 to have it proved to my satisfaction that there is no such place as hell". His conscience was waking up to proclaim in that solemn hour that sins must be followed by the judgment of God. Where death leaves you judgment will find you, and the issue of that judgment will be final and for eternity.

How will you die? The Spirit of God has written a short but solemn epitaph in Hebrews 10:28. God forbid that it should ever be true of my reader! Here it is

"DIED WITHOUT MERCY".

An innocent man might plead for justice, but *the sinner's* only hope is *mercy*. The guilty one can only escape by the door of *mercy*. If the offender does not receive the due reward of his deeds, it must be on the ground of *mercy*. The transgressor can only be pardoned at the *mercy-seat*. Hence the penitent's cry is, "God be *merciful* to me a sinner"; he is conscious that nothing but *mercy* will do for him. Your only chance is *mercy*. Oh! how sad, how complete, how irretrievable will be your ruin, if you die "*without mercy*"!

There is another epitaph - short but blessed - in Hebrews 11:13. Look at it!

"THESE ALL DIED IN FAITH".

Yes! though the men thus spoken of lived in a dispensation of comparative darkness - though they had not a love-provided Saviour, or a fully finished atoning work to rest upon - yet in the starlight of types, symbols, and promises they trod the path of *faith*, which is now lighted up for us by the glory which shines in the face of the seated Saviour on the throne of God, and as they lived so they died - "*in faith*".

God has not been indifferent to the ruin of His creature, whose sin has brought death upon him. There is no denying the fact "that the wages of sin is death", but it is equally true that "the *gift of God* is eternal life through Jesus Christ our Lord" (Romans 6:23. "In this was manifested *the love of God* toward us, because that God sent his only begotten Son into the world, that we might *live through him*" (1 John 4:9). The holy Son of God has upon the cross. Yea, God commends His love to us, in that, while we were yet sinners, *Christ died for us.* The old preacher never spoke so loudly, or in such solemn tones, as when Jesus went to Calvary. Divine love would bless the sinner, but divine holiness could not make light of the sin. The full penalty of guilt - the wages of sin in all its dark and dread reality - passed upon the sinless Substitute. He took our place in death and judgment, that we might have His life and His place of acceptance and favour before God.

> *"Oh! for this love let rocks and hills*
> *Their lasting silence break;*
> *And all harmonious, human tongues*
> *The Saviour's praises speak!"*

You may die *unsaved*; you will not die *unloved*. The Son of God is for you: Christ died for you: eternal life may be yours. The love of God - the work of Christ - the Spirit's strivings, all urge you to turn from the world and its delusions, which end in *death*, to the Son of God whose soul-assuring words are - "He that heareth my word, and believeth on him that sent me, hath everlasting life, and shall not come into judgment; but is passed *from death unto life*" (John 5:24).

Love's pleading voice echoes every solemn warning of the old preacher, but adds in compassionate tenderness the gracious inquiry,

"*Why will ye die*?" It is true that you can never regain the paradise of Eden, or reach that tree whose fruit would give perpetuity to your present life on earth. All that is connected with the first creation - now ruined by sin - must pass away. But the love of God has revealed a fairer and brighter scene than Eden; a more glorious paradise than that of man's innocence has been opened up by the death of Jesus. The joys of heaven, the endless festivities of the Father's house, the love of the Father's heart and eternal glory in companionship with the Son of God, may all be yours.

Nor are the Christian's blessings all in the future. He is brought to God *now*, and knows God as the Source of all his blessing; he has the Holy Spirit; he walks by the Spirit in fellowship with God, and tastes thus of heaven's delights before he gets there; death casts no shadow on his blessings, for they are wrapped up in One who is alive from the dead, and connected with a scene where death can never come; in spirit he lives already on the other side of death: in short, he *has* passed "*from death unto life*".

Then, if he "falls asleep" and is "absent from the body", it is to be "present with the Lord". Death is no loss to the child of God, but an infinite gain. It frees him from the presence of sin, and from a body which groans under the bondage of corruption, and he departs to be "with Christ, which is *far better*".

Best of all, Jesus is coming soon to receive His own to Himself, and at His shout the dead in Christ shall rise first, and then we which are alive and remain shall be changed and caught up into glory *without dying at all* (see Philippians 3:20-21; 1 Corinthians 15:51; 1 Thessalonians 4:16-17).

ARE YOU READY?

The nearness of the coming of the Lord Jesus Christ is being pressed on many hearts at the present time. Many children of God believe that we are living in the critical and solemn moments which immediately precede the coming of the bridegroom. This momentous event - fraught with unspeakable consequences to both saint and sinner - is brought before our consideration by the Spirit of God in the parable of the ten virgins.

"Then shall the kingdom of heaven be likened unto ten virgins, which took their lamps, and went forth to meet the bridegroom. And five of them were wise, and five were foolish. They that were foolish took their lamps, and took no oil with them: but the wise took oil in their vessels with their lamps. While the bridegroom tarried they all slumbered and slept. And at midnight there was a cry made, Behold, the bridegroom cometh, go ye out to meet him. Then all those virgins arose, and trimmed their lamps. And the foolish said unto the wise, Give us of your oil; for our lamps are gone out. But the wise answered, saying, Not so; lest there be not enough for us and you: but go ye rather to them that sell, and buy for yourselves. And while they went to buy, the bridegroom came; and they that were ready went in with him to the marriage;

and the door was shut. Afterward came also the other virgins, saying, Lord, Lord, open to us. But he answered and said, Verily I say unto you, I know you not. Watch therefore, for ye know neither the day nor the hour wherein the Son of man cometh" (Matthew 25:1-13).

The kingdom of heaven embraces all who take the ground of Christian profession; it includes all who own that Jesus is Lord, and who receive the truths of Christianity. But amongst the many who take this ground there are tares, bad fish which will have to be thrown away, foolish virgins, and wicked servants. They are in the place of privilege and responsibility as professing to own Christ as Lord and assenting to the truths of the Christian faith, but they have no vital and saving knowledge of the Lord Jesus Christ.

We are in the midst of a professedly Christian people; the Bible is taught in our schools, and found almost universally in our homes. An oath upon the Scriptures is recognised as the most solemn safeguard against untruth in the courts of law. But these very facts make it all the more necessary that we should recognise the immense difference which subsists between the foolish virgins and the wise. It is surely of the highest importance that we should consider seriously whether we ourselves are amongst the wise.

A moment draws near which will effectually

and for ever separate the foolish from the wise; but it will then be too late to consider or repent. I beseech you now, therefore, while it is called today, to give earnest attention to this solemn matter.

In Scripture the number ten is connected with human responsibility. For example, there are ten commandments in the law. So here the ten virgins represent the responsible Christian profession on earth. We are told they "went forth to meet the bridegroom". When the gospel was first proclaimed in the world large numbers received it, and came out from Judaism and heathendom "to serve the living and true God, and to wait for his Son from heaven". All Christians professedly "went forth to meet the bridegroom".

But, though outwardly alike, and animated apparently by the same motives, Christians have from the first been composed of two classes. Many have, like Simon in Acts 8, believed and been baptised, of whom it might be truly said that they have had "neither part nor lot in this matter".

Lookers-on might discern no difference and make no distinction between the virgins. All might be apparelled in the same festal robes, and all might carry lamps of the same kind. But five of them were lacking in the most essential point. They "took no oil with them". The most magnificent oil-lamp in the world without oil is absolutely useless for any practical purpose. And of what value is a profession of Christianity, if the soul is not really converted to God? It may serve for a time to silence the voice of conscience and to deceive a foolish heart, but in the solemn hour for which nothing will avail but divine reality it will be found altogether worthless.

Throughout Scripture oil is a type of the Holy Spirit, and the essential difference between the wise and foolish virgins is that one class have the Holy Spirit and the other have not. All the true grace and power of Christianity is connected with the Holy Spirit, and if a man has not the Holy Spirit he must be a stranger to it all. Believers are not only born again by the Spirit, but they receive the Spirit as an indwelling Person. This is of such vital importance that we must enlarge a little upon it.

The gift of the Holy Spirit is consequent upon redemption being accomplished. It was not until Jesus had died and risen and been glorified at the right hand of God that the Holy Spirit was given. No saint on earth was ever *indwelt* by the Holy Spirit before the ascension of Christ. Prophets and holy men of God had been moved and energised by Him to an extraordinary degree, but they were not permanently indwelt by the Spirit. John 7:39 tells us that "the Holy Ghost was not yet given, because that Jesus was not yet glorified". But now redemption has been accomplished, and the One who wrought it has been exalted to the right hand of God, and from that glorified One the Holy Spirit has come down to dwell in those who believe on Him, and who know through grace the efficacy of His finished work.

There are many persons in whom God has wrought conviction of sin, and who are in a certain way looking to Jesus for salvation, who do not know what it is to be justified. In many cases this is because they have never heard the full, clear gospel of the grace of God. They have not received the Spirit because they have not yet accepted by faith the Lord Jesus and His finished work as all their salvation. If they did so it would set their souls for ever at rest, and the Holy Spirit would seal them, for He is here to seal those who receive the word of truth, the gospel of their salvation (Ephesians 1:13).

If you are a believer on the Lord Jesus, and yet have not perfect peace with God, it is clear that you have only received part of the gospel. The Lord Jesus has been "delivered for our offences" (Romans 4:25). He has borne our sins, and removed all the judgment that was due to them by bearing it in His own body on the tree. He has been made sin for us, and in our place and condemnation He - the just and Holy One - has glorified God. We were subject to the sentence of death according to divine justice. He has come under that sentence for us according to divine grace. He has thus settled every question, and silenced every accusing voice.

But He has also been "raised again for our justification". The Lord Jesus has been placed by God's resurrection power beyond the reach of sin, judgment, or death. No power of evil can touch Him, death hath no more dominion over Him, no shade or cloud can ever come upon His acceptance with God. Man - in the person of Christ risen - is in a place of cloudless and eternal favour before God. But He was "raised again *for our justification*". He holds that place on behalf of all who believe on His name. He holds it that we may learn in Him the measure of our righteousness and acceptance with God. Through infinite divine grace that risen and glorified One is the righteousness of every believer.

It is the justified believer, the one who knows the risen Christ as his righteousness, who receives the Spirit. It is on the ground that our righteousness and acceptance are *perfect* that we receive the Spirit. Not that *we* are perfect, or indeed anything but guilty and lost sinners, but Christ has borne all the judgment that was due to us, so that He might be our righteousness, and HE is perfect. The Spirit is given because of what Christ is, He is given to shed the love of God abroad in the believer's heart, and to make us conscious of the favour in which we are set by divine grace.

Now let me ask, do you know anything of this? Is Christ your righteousness? Have you received the Spirit? Have you oil in your vessel? The foolish virgins "*took no oil with them*".

We need not dwell upon the statement that "while the bridegroom tarried they all slumbered and slept". It will suffice to say that scarcely had the apostle John been laid in his grave, about the end of the first century, when the promise of the absent One was forgotten; the church ceased to look for Christ's return. Wise and foolish virgins alike slumbered and slept. An awful slumber of indifference to the absent but coming bridegroom settled down upon the church for long centuries.

It is evident that such a state of things could not be allowed to continue until the bridegroom came. God - jealous for the glory of His Son, and mindful of what was due to the coming One - would have the sleeping virgins roused. And to this end, "At midnight there was a cry made, Behold the bridegroom, go ye out to meet him".

More than a century ago God graciously revived "that blessed hope" amongst His children, and truths connected with the coming of the Lord were published far and wide. There can be no doubt that the midnight cry has gone forth. Many thousands have been awakened thereby, and there has been to a considerable extent a trimming of lamps and a going forth to meet the bridegroom.

It is certain that we are living at the present moment in the interval between the shout that heralds the bridegroom's approach and His actual arrival. The exact moment of His coming is unknown, but it cannot now be long delayed. It is of vital importance to be *ready*. Those who know the grace of God, whose sins are forgiven, and who are indwelt and led by the Spirit are *ready*. Is it not high time to awake and trim your lamp?

"Give us of your oil", say the foolish virgins to the wise, "for our lamps are going out". What a discovery to make when the bridegroom is at hand! Of what avail are the forms and privileges of a religious life, or the cherished dogmas of an orthodox creed, or moral comeliness which may be irreproachable in the eyes of men, if the heart is not illuminated with divine grace, as possessing righteousness in Christ and having the Spirit of adoption whereby we cry, Abba, Father? Lacking this, Christianity is an empty shell - an oil-less lamp - it is really Christianity *without Christ*.

Nor can the wise share their oil with the foolish. The children of believing parents, the husbands of believing wives, the near and dear relatives of God's people, must go for themselves to buy. Thank God, there is still space for repentance and for faith. The day of salvation lingers, and it is still the accepted time. But great is the peril of delay.

"While they went to buy the bridegroom came". How solemn to think of this! Souls awakened, interested, exercised, and apparently moving in the right direction, but *not ready* when the bridegroom came, and therefore shut out for judgment. It is possible that you may have been awakened to some measure of concern about your soul, you may be to some extent interested in the gospel, and Satan would fain persuade you that because you have these good desires and better feelings you are sure to be all right at last. Be not deceived. You are very likely to be left behind for judgment and the lake of fire. Nothing short of the knowledge and reception by faith of the Lord Jesus Christ will avail. There is no security until you know Him as all your salvation.

"And they that were ready went in with him to the marriage: and the door was shut. Afterward came also the other virgins, saying, Lord, Lord, open to us. But he answered and said, Verily I say unto you, I know you not". Today this is *prophecy*; tomorrow it may be *history*. Tomorrow the redeemed company, sanctified by the Holy Spirit, may have gone in with the bridegroom. Tomorrow the door of access to Christ - so widely open now - may be shut. Then the unsanctified professor of religion, destitute of faith in Christ, ignorant of the grace of God, and having not the Spirit, will be outside and unknown by the Lord.

In view of this solemn event, with all its stupendous issues, and in view also of the fact that it may take place at any moment - in such an hour as ye think not - let me ask again, *are you ready*?

A COMMON AND PRESENT SALVATION

Everybody knows that a common is a piece of ground open to all, and to which no one has an exclusive right. One of the chief glories of the salvation of God, which He is sending to the Gentiles in this day of grace, is that it is a "common salvation" (Jude 3). Not restricted or confined to any particular class, but presented to all, not as a reward of merit, or as wages in return for a certain amount of work, but as a free gift to sinners whose common ruin and need makes them require a "common salvation".

Many people greatly disliked the preaching of a "common salvation". It might be thought that the announcement of a salvation available for *all* was a generous display of divine grace which must secure the admiration of every heart. But such is not the case, and the reason is not difficult to find. If God provides salvation for all it must be because *all are lost.* If only *some* had been lost, there would have been no need to provide salvation for *all.* "The grace of God that bringeth salvation to all men hath appeared". High and low, rich and poor, learned and ignorant, refined and depraved, sensitive and sensual find themselves here on a *common* level, and God writes over them

"All have sinned and come short of the glory of God".

This is an unwelcome truth to man's proud heart, because it tears every rag of human righteousness to tatters, makes an end of human boasting, and puts the extinguisher on every spark of human pride. That a poor slave of Satan who was steeped in lust and crime was a lost sinner many would be free to admit; but few really consider that a moral, decent, respectable, and religious man is also a lost sinner. Yet both classes stand on precisely the same platform before God. It is written, "There is no difference, for *all* have sinned and come short of the glory of God". No doubt there was a great difference between people in Noah's day, as far as their character and conduct went, but there was no difference as to their state before God. Outside the ark all perished. Just so in the night of Egypt's judgment. Some of the Egyptians might be very wicked and others very moral, but there was no difference in respect to the destroying angel. The firstborn died in every house where the blood of the lamb was not sprinkled. The fact of a common salvation being provided proves that there is a common need. From the King on his throne to the beggar in his wayside cabin - prince, peer, and peasant - all alike are involved in the same condemnation, and, if saved at all, must be saved by the "common salvation".

We have a beautiful and very simple type of

this in Exodus 30:15. In many of the other offerings a man might give according to his ability, and as his heart stirred him up - consequently the rich were able to give greater offerings than the poor - but every distinction was levelled down when the atonement offering was in question. The rich might not give more than half a shekel, and the poor might not give less. The half-shekel offering was common to all the tribes of Israel.

Then the grand question is, Where can this "common salvation" be found? and how can a sinner become possessed of it? Let us read Acts 16:30-31. The jailor "brought them out, and said, Sirs, what must I do to be saved? and they said, Believe on the Lord Jesus Christ, and thou shalt be saved, and thy house". Here was an anxious sinner - one who wanted to be saved - and mark the simplicity of the direction given him by the apostle: "Believe on the Lord Jesus Christ, and thou shalt be saved". Salvation is wrapped up in a Person. "God so loved the world that he gave his only begotten Son", and Simeon took up the infant Jesus - a babe of six weeks - saying, "Now, Lord, lettest thou thy servant depart in peace according to thy word, for mine eyes have seen *thy salvation*" (Luke 2:25-32) More than thirty years afterwards Jesus said, as He entered the house of Zacchæus, the rich publican of Jericho, "This day is salvation come to this house". The Lord Jesus Christ, having accomplished the work of redemption, and having been exalted to the very throne whose claims He has vindicated with His blood, is presented to us as the salvation of God, "neither is there salvation in any other". Nothing more than Christ is needed by the vilest sinner who breathes God's air, and nothing less than Christ will avail for the most decent sinner in the world. This is the "common salvation". It is provided by God; it is wrapped up in the Lord Jesus Christ; and it is for any sinner who will accept it.

PRESENT SALVATION

Salvation is a present thing. It is something to be received and enjoyed *now*. It is sad to see so many hearing the gospel, who put it away from them time after time, because their convenient season has not come. It is God's convenient season now. He says, Come *now*, and let us reason together: though your sins be scarlet, they shall be white as snow; though they be red like crimson, they shall be as wool.

God is at the present moment a justifier and a Saviour God, but those who make light of His grace will be destroyed. In the parable of the great supper the invitation went out, "Come, for all things are now ready". But the guests were not ready. "They all with one consent began to make excuse", and the insulted giver of the feast uttered the solemn words, "None of those men which were bidden shall taste of my supper".

Then do not put off this question. The Spaniards have a proverb that the road of By-and-by leads to the town of Never. An old writer said that procrastination was the recruiting officer of hell. Thousands are now in hell who fully intended to be saved. But they trifled with their opportunities, and neglected salvation until it was too late.

Thank God, it is not yet too late for the reader of this book. "Behold, Now is the accepted time; behold, now is the day of salvation" (2 Corinthians 6:2). "Today, if ye will hear his voice, harden not your hearts".

Then the salvation of God is a present salvation, because its benefits are to be enjoyed now. Two things are essential to salvation - the forgiveness of sins and the knowledge of God; and both are present things. When a man says that it is not possible to have the knowledge of salvation in this world, you may be sure of one thing, that he has it not himself. If a blind man were to say that nobody could see, or a deaf man were to say that nobody could hear, we should pity their misfortune and smile at their folly. And when we hear people say that it is impossible in this life to be saved and know it, we can only regard it as an evidence of their own unhappy state, and a practical confession that they are strangers to grace and to God. When human opinions are laid aside, and the gracious testimony of God in His glad tidings received, all uncertainty departs from the soul. The Saviour of whom the Bible speaks is a real Saviour, and the blessings which He imparts to those who believe on Him are present realities. Faith enjoys them now; doubt and uncertainty are the miserable children of that guilty parent - unbelief. The knowledge of salvation is, through grace, the portion of the believer.

"To give knowledge of salvation unto his people, by the remission of their sins" (Luke 1:77). The way in which God approaches men in grace is entirely consistent with Himself, but it is also divinely suited to the guilty condition in which men are found. The only possible way in which God could approach men in grace is as "a God ready to pardon" (Nehemiah 9:17). Our first knowledge of Him must be in this character. We could have no relations with God in grace except on the ground of the remission of sins. We are justly chargeable with the guilt of many sins, but God has taken this into account, and His grace meets us with full and free forgiveness.

Yet the ground on which the proclamation of forgiveness is based forbids the thought that there is unrighteousness, or indifference to sin, with God. Grace reigns indeed, but reigns through righteousness. "The man Christ Jesus ... gave himself a ransom for all" (1 Timothy 2:6), and it is because He has "once suffered for sins, the just for the unjust", that "repentance and remission of sins" are "preached in his name among all nations" (Luke 24:47). Those who receive the forgiveness thus proclaimed obtain the "knowledge of salvation ... by the remission of their sins". They are brought to the knowledge of God in grace, and they rejoice in Him as the God of their salvation.

Then in Hebrews 5:9 we read of

"ETERNAL SALVATION".

Many souls are robbed of peace and joy because they have no assurance of eternal security. They find such weakness in themselves that they cannot be sure that they will endure unto the end. Such an exercise is not without value if it leads to absolute self-distrust, and constrains the soul to "cleave with purpose of heart unto the Lord". All our security as saints is in divine Persons, and the more entirely our hearts are assured of this, the more free shall we be from doubts and fears.

If we have started out in Christian profession by an act of our own will, we may depart from it in like manner. But if God has by His Spirit convicted us of sin, and called us by the gospel to the knowledge of Himself and of His Son Jesus Christ our Lord, we are conscious that we owe all to His grace and sovereign mercy. We have neither goodness, strength, security, nor blessing of any kind *in ourselves*. God has been pleased to make Himself known to us as a justifier and a Saviour God, and all the blessing that He has given us is secured in Christ risen, "who of God is made unto us wisdom, and righteousness, and sanctification, and redemption that, according as it is written, he that glorieth, let him glory in the Lord" (1 Corinthians 1:30-31).

And God, having thus secured blessing for us in Christ Jesus, "shall also confirm you unto the end, that ye may be blameless in the day of our Lord Jesus Christ" (1 Corinthians 1:8). "He which hath begun a good work in you, will perform it until the day of Jesus Christ" (Philippians 1:6). God's designs of grace and sovereign mercy do not break down. "Whom he did predestinate, them he also called: and whom he called, them he also justified: and whom he justified, them he also glorified" (Romans 8:30).

We need not only to be assured by knowing the stability of God's eternal purpose, but we need practical security from all the power of evil along the pathway here. There is a tremendous power of evil here, but Christ knows it all. He has met it and triumphed over it, and now, as risen and glorified, He has become "the author of eternal salvation unto all them that obey him". He, and He alone, can carry His people through, with suited grace for each hour of need. If we attempt to tread the path of faith in self-confidence we are sure to break down. If we realise our total weakness and cleave to Him, He will not fail to succour and sustain us. Our security lies in the fact that we are conscious of having no strength or resources in ourselves, but that we have all support and succour in One who cannot fail us. He says, "My sheep hear my voice, and I know them, and they follow me: and I give unto them eternal life; and they shall never perish, neither shall any pluck them out of my hand" (John 10:27, 28). "Now unto him that is able to keep from falling, and to present you faultless before the presence of his glory with exceeding joy, to the only wise God our Saviour, be glory and majesty, dominion and power, both now and ever. Amen" (Jude 24-25).

THE GREAT SALVATION

God has provided salvation for man; a salvation which is adapted to the necessities of the vilest sinner on earth; a salvation, too, which the moral and respectable cannot afford to be without; and a salvation which, while it comes down to the lowest depths of human need, is in perfect harmony with all the high and holy attributes of God. Yea, it is a salvation which not only brings eternal blessing to the sinner, but secures eternal glory to God Himself. It is rightly called a "great salvation" (Hebrews 2:3), and we may well affirm that it is so when we think of

THE GREAT NEED WHICH IT MEETS.

Nothing could be more pitiable than the condition of an unsaved sinner. His conscience is not at rest, for he cannot altogether forget his sins, and death and judgment loom darkly ahead. His heart is unsatisfied, for he has nothing but the world as his portion, and it gives no lasting peace or joy; its sweetest cup of pleasure is soured by the dregs of disappointment. Verily it must be a *great salvation* which will meet all his need, remove his fears, give peace to his conscience before God, and satisfy his heart.

No doubt many might say, "But I have felt no

need of this kind. It is true I do not like to think of death and judgment, and I am free to admit that it makes me feel uncomfortable to hear people talk about such subjects, but at other times I feel happy and content. I am quite satisfied with the world". My friend, I linger to have a word with you. It is fearful to be *unsaved*, but a sinner unsaved and *unconcerned* is one of the saddest and most appalling spectacles which the world can present. It is sad to be afflicted with disease, but infinitely worse to have some deep-seated malady undermining and destroying your constitution without being aware of the fact. Let your thoughts dwell for a moment on the gravity of your position. However lightly you think of your sins, and however little you are troubled about them, unless they are washed away by the atoning blood of Christ they will be your eternal destruction. If you die in your sins you will certainly spend eternity in the lake of fire. Does this disturb the peace of your mind? I hope it does. It is far better to be disturbed in this world than to be damned in the next. May God awaken you even now from your slumber of indifference, and cause you to apply yourself in earnest to the consideration of the all-important question - "What must I do to be saved?"

To one who has felt his need, and has groaned beneath the weight of sin, the tidings of a great salvation is a pleasant sound; to his troubled and anxious heart it comes like balm of Gilead to soothe and heal. For, as before remarked; it, is worthy to be called a *great* salvation, because there is no sinner whose need it is not able to meet. Satan has two great lies which he uses - oftentimes, alas! with conspicuous success - to destroy the souls of men. First, he persuades them that they do not need salvation; they are so good, their character so upright, their morality of such a high tone, and their religious profession of such a degree, that they have no need to come as guilty rebels to God to receive mercy like common sinners. But by the grace of God, in spite of this satanic lie, sinners do become anxious and alarmed. God speaks to their consciences by His Word and Spirit, and they become exercised about their state before Him. Then Satan has another lie ready for them, exactly opposite to the former one. He turns round and says, "Consider what sins you have committed! Remember how you have treated God! how you have scoffed at His mercy and refused His grace, and gone on taking pleasure in your sins in spite of all His warnings and entreaties! How can you expect to be saved? There may be mercy for others, but not for you".

Thus he seeks to plunge the trembling sinner into despair. But how the "great salvation" confronts and confounds him! There is no sinner with crimes of so deep a dye, with guilt so aggravated, with need so great, that he is beyond the reach of this *great* salvation. Yea, the greater the sinner, the more is God's grace magnified in saving him. Let not your heart be discouraged then, if you have felt your guiltiness before a holy God, and have even, perhaps, been caused to doubt whether His salvation could extend to one so vile as you. A Magdalene, a dying thief, a brutal Philippian jailor, and the arch-persecutor of the saints, Saul of Tarsus - chief of sinners - bear eloquent witness to the greatness of God's salvation. If sin abounds, grace much more abounds, and those who have been brought up from the lowest depths of sin and shame will be the brightest monuments of the exceeding riches of God's abounding grace.

Then, again, the salvation of which the apostle speaks is

GREAT BECAUSE OF ITS SOURCE.

It is the "salvation of God" (Acts 28:28). If we would learn the full measure of its greatness, we must follow it to its source, and see it flowing forth in streams of eternal blessing from the heart of God Himself. "For God so loved the world, that he gave his only begotten Son, that whosoever believeth in him should not perish, but have everlasting life" (John 3:16). How these precious words unfold to us the heart of God! How they cause us to wonder and adore at the wealth of love bestowed by Him upon undeserving men! Truly "in this was manifested the love of God toward us, because that God sent his only begotten Son into the world, that we might live through him". I should like to know the wealth of love that is wrapped up in those words - "*his well-beloved*" (Mark 12:6). *He* it was who was given as the manifestation and expression of God's love to this world. Herein lies the glory of that salvation of which we speak. It proceeds from God Himself. It was He who loved, it was He who gave His Son, and it is He who has pledged His word for the salvation of every sinner who believes on that heaven-sent Saviour. It is all of God from first to last. Then cease every effort to attain salvation by doings of your own; labour not in the vain attempt to make yourself acceptable to God by moral reformation, or by attendance to religious duties, but come and learn the infinite grace of God, and join with us who have known and believed it in praising Him for His great salvation.

Further, this is a *great* salvation

BECAUSE OF THE INFINITE COST

at which it has been procured. We do well to remember that though salvation is offered to us without money and without price, in the largeness and liberality of the grace of God, it has been procured at an infinite cost. And this we must realise if we consider that before God could save a sinner He must be able to do it in accordance with His own righteousness and holiness, as well as in the activity of His mercy and grace. If God issued a general pardon to all sinners, irrespective of satisfaction rendered to Him on account of their sins, where would be His truth, His righteousness, His holiness?

God cannot pass over sin in the free-and-easy way so common among men. He must punish sin; and the grand problem which had to be solved before there could be salvation for guilty sinners was how the sin might be judged, and at the same time the sinner saved. How could this be done? In no other way than by the Son of God going to the cross, and there bearing the judgment of God upon sin. I am bold to say, with most profound reverence, that the salvation of a sinner, consistently with divine righteousness, was a work which taxed the utmost resources of God. To accomplish this His beloved Son must, as the Son of man, be lifted up upon the cross. That blessed One must suffer, or He could not save. The throne from which God extends the golden sceptre of salvation to repentant sinners does not stand upon the ruins of justice. Grace reigns indeed, but through righteousness, and God is just in justifying the ungodly sinner who believes in Jesus. The holiness of God has found that which met all its claims in the death of Christ, and divine righteousness has been fully vindicated by that one offering whereby the sins of believers were for ever put away. But think of the darkness of that midnight-noon which for three hours enwrapped the Saviour in its gloomy shades. Think of the depth of anguish which wrung from His heart that bitter wail of grief, "My God, my God, why hast thou forsaken me?" What untold travail of soul did He pass through before He could proclaim that His great redemption work was "finished!"

As we contemplate that scene - and may we stand, in figure, with unshod feet as we do so, for the ground is thrice holy - we learn something of what sin is in the sight of God. No sacrifice of meaner rank could satisfy the lofty requirements of divine righteousness; the blood of no other victim possessed the needed efficacy to cleanse the sinner from his scarlet stains of guilt.

Then again, this salvation is *great* by reason of the

GREAT BLESSINGS

which it confers. I may briefly mention three. (1) "Whosoever believeth in him shall receive remission of sins" (Acts 10:43). The believer rejoices in a present known forgiveness. He waits not for the day of judgment to be assured of full clearance; he knows that his "sins are forgiven" (1 John 2:12); they have been cast into the depths of that sea of divine judgment whose billows rolled over Jesus at Calvary, and from those depths they can never rise. God has said, "Their sins and iniquities will I remember no more" (Hebrews 10:17). Such is the efficacy of the "one sacrifice for sins" which Christ has offered. It has secured eternal redemption and a purged conscience for every believer.

(2) "Being justified by faith, we have peace with God through our Lord Jesus Christ" (Romans 5:1). The believer's standing with God is measured by Christ risen, for He has been "raised again for our justification" (Romans 4:25). No charge can ever be brought against Him - death and judgment can never more pass upon Him - He is in everlasting righteousness with God. And by God's pure grace we are set in His standing and acceptance. The knowledge of this fills the soul with divine and changeless peace.

(3) "The love of God is shed abroad in our hearts by the Holy Ghost which is given unto us" (Romans 5:5). The Holy Spirit has been sent down from a glorified Saviour, and the first part of His wonderful mission is to fulfil this precious verse for the believer, and it is thus that the joy of salvation comes into the heart.

Now pause a moment, and consider whether a salvation which can meet the need of the vilest, and which flows from such a source as the heart of God, and through such a channel as the sufferings and death of His beloved Son, and a salvation which results in such infinite blessings to those who accept it, is not worthy to be called

If we admit that it is so, with what solemn force does the inspired question come home to our souls - "How shall we escape, if we neglect so great salvation?" When such glorious provision has been made, when such unbounded stores of love and grace have been thrown open, when such appeals and invitations have been sent forth, what shall the end be of those who persist in neglecting *such* a salvation?

This solemn question is most wholesome to consider, but it is hopelessly unanswerable. No fiend in hell, no angel from before the throne of God, can frame an answer to it. On the other hand, there is the solemn declaration of God recorded in 1 Thessalonians 5, "*They shall not escape*". How could it be possible to escape after refusing God's love, despising His grace, rejecting His Son, scorning His mercy, and defying His justice? And all this and more is involved in the neglect of His great salvation.

Think not to avail yourself of the paltry plea that you have never positively *rejected* salvation, and that you mean to be saved some day. If unsaved at this moment you are a *neglecter* of God's salvation, and the question before us is, "How shall we escape, if we *neglect* so great salvation?" May the Holy Spirit impress these words upon your heart and keep them ringing in your ears until you realise in the depths of your being that there can be *no escape* for those who neglect Christ.

Why should you neglect Him? He is willing and mighty to save, and has said for the encouragement of sinners, “Him that cometh to me I will in no wise cast out”. You hope to be finally saved: why not *now*? You hope that in the eternity to which we haste your voice will swell the anthems and doxologies of the heavenly host: why not sing the redemption song *today*? “If thou shalt confess with thy mouth the Lord Jesus, and shalt believe in thine heart that God hath raised him from the dead, thou shalt be saved”.

WORDS OF SALVATION

"Words whereby thou and all thy house shall be saved", Acts 11:14

God is not willing that you should perish, or that you should remain under the bondage of sin or the law, and He directs you to certain words whereby you and your house may be saved - saved from the wrath to come, from the power of Satan, and from the world; saved for glory, for the eternal company of Christ in the Father's house, and for the life and liberty of divine grace here on earth. Dear reader, would you not like to have this wonderful blessing? You are surely conscious that you need something you have not got. The world with its fleeting pleasures has failed to satisfy your heart, and many a stain of sin is upon your soul. Will you not listen with living interest to words of salvation? You may have *security* which no storm of infernal wrath can ever impair - which no decree of divine judgment will ever assail; you may have undisturbed and everlasting *peace*; you may have joy, compared with which all earthly joys are times of mourning. What a glorious train of blessing - all consequent upon certain "words" whereby you and your house may be saved!

An anxious sinner may find great comfort in the case of Cornelius, to whom these words of salvation were addressed by Peter (see Acts

10). If you partake of his anxiety you will assuredly partake of his blessing. It may not come to you quite in the same manner as it came to him. No angelic messenger is likely to wing his rapid flight from the shores of everlasting bliss to direct you. Nor is such guidance necessary or desirable, for the very words which in olden time fell on the ears of Cornelius are still preserved by the Spirit of God. They are still God's message to every anxious soul, and they are still able to make "wise unto salvation".

Then let us learn from Cornelius the way in which God's message should be received. Speaking to Peter, he says, "*immediately* therefore I sent to thee" (Acts 10:33). Have you such a sense of your need as to wish for an immediate settlement of this great question? There is incalculable peril in delay, and the issues at stake are too tremendous to be trifled with. The possibility of lying under the judgment of God for ever is so fearful, that to contemplate it for a single moment ought to be sufficient to awaken in the heart of every sinner an intense desire to hear "immediately" words whereby he may be saved.

Then, notice, it was to God that Cornelius turned as the only source of blessing. It was true that he had sent for Peter as the appointed channel of blessing, but he says distinctly, "Now therefore are we all here present *before God*, to hear all things that are commanded thee *of God*" (verse 33). We see, then, three things in Cornelius. He was a man (1) who knew his need of salvation; (2) who wished to be saved "immediately"; and (3) who was before God as one whose expectation was alone from God. If my reader is like-minded, I can answer for it that he will obtain blessing.

Let us then, as in the very presence of God, listen to these "words" of Peter: "*Of a truth I perceive that God is no respecter of persons*" (Acts 10:34).

It was a great thing for Peter to say this. He had had to learn, as we read in this chapter, that the grace of God was above all ceremonial and external distinctions. God would as readily, in His grace, make a Gentile clean as a Jew. It had pleased Him, for special reasons, to separate the Jew from the Gentile, and to confer privileges on the former which were not possessed by the latter, but there was "no difference" in the sight of God between them. Both were alike sinners, and could only be blessed by the grace of God. The religious Jew thought himself very much better than the profane Gentile, but in truth it was not so. His position and privileges only added to his responsibility.

It is still true that God is no respecter of persons. God is not influenced by the distinctions and differences which prevail in society and in the religious world. An unconverted bishop is just the same before the eye of God as an unconverted sexton; one has a high place in the religious world, and the other a very humble place, but in the eye of God they are both lost sinners on their way to hell. On the other hand, a shoeblack exercised about his soul would be as great an object of interest to God as a monarch who was in the same anxiety. God has concluded all under sin, and it is on this common platform alone that He approaches sinners in His wondrous grace.

"*But in every nation he that feareth him, and worketh righteousness, is accepted with him*" (Acts 10: 35).

"The fear of the Lord is the beginning of wisdom", and whenever a soul bows in the fear of God, and acknowledges his own worthlessness and ruin before God, he is in a condition upon which God can look with pleasure. His working of righteousness is not the proud activity of a legal spirit, but the lowly bringing forth of "fruits meet for repentance", and he is "accepted" with God. "There is joy in the presence of the angels of God over one sinner that repenteth". The sinner is now in the state of one who will rejoice to hear of sovereign mercy and redeeming grace.

"*The word which God sent unto the children of Israel, preaching peace by Jesus Christ: (he is Lord of all)*" (Acts 10: 36).

This sentence introduces us at once to the

presence of the Saviour; it attests His divine authority, proclaims His mission, and asserts the dignity of His Person. The Son of God came from heaven not to pour out the vengeance of an angry God upon a guilty race, but to preach peace to them. Well may angels wonder and adore! Well may the redeemed hosts proclaim His praises with eternal hallelujahs!

"*That word, I say, ye know, which was published throughout all Judæa, and began from Galilee, after the baptism which John preached; how God anointed Jesus of Nazareth with the Holy Ghost and with power: who went about doing good, and healing all that were oppressed of the devil; for God was with him. And we are witnesses of all things which he did, both in the land of the Jews, and in Jerusalem; whom they slew and hanged on a tree*" (Acts 10: 37-39).

Think of that blessed One - the anointed One of God, the Missionary of peace, the doer of good, the One with whom God was, the Lord of all - being *slain and hanged on a tree*! Surely man's enmity to God could go no further. Man has shown himself in his true colours. He became a sinner in Eden and a transgressor at Sinai, but at Calvary we see him as the open enemy of God - the red-handed murderer of God's beloved Son. How marvellous that in this very scene of man's blackest crime and most malignant enmity to God we see shining out in eternal splendour the rays of God's transcendent grace and love to man!

"Inscribed upon the cross we see
In shining letters, God is love".

How truly may we apply Joseph's words to the cross of Christ: "As for you, ye thought evil against me; but God meant it unto good, to bring to pass, as it is this day, to save much people alive" (Genesis 50:20). If men by wicked hands crucified and slew the Lord's Anointed, it was nevertheless true that He laid down His life by the Father's commandment, to glorify God in making atonement for sin, so that on the ground of His death repentance and remission of sins might be preached in His name among all nations, beginning at Jerusalem. And "God commendeth his love toward us, in that, while we were yet sinners, Christ died for us" (Romans 5:8).

"*Him God raised up the third day, and shewed him openly; not to all the people, but unto witnesses chosen before of God, even to us, who did eat and drink with him after he rose from the dead*" (Acts 10: 40-41).

The death of Christ was no triumph for Satan; it was a mighty victory for God; and on the morning of the third day the risen Lord stepped forth Conqueror of death and the grave. Satan's machinations were eternally frustrated; man's impotent wickedness had raged only to accomplish the will of God. Well might all heaven break forth in a swelling shout of triumphant acclamation to greet the risen and victorious Saviour! “Lift up your heads, O ye gates; and be ye lift up, ye everlasting doors; and the king of glory shall come in”.

After such a work accomplished - after such a victory won - after such a Person has been in such a place - we are not surprised to hear the words fall from Peter’s lips -

“*To him give all the prophets witness, that through his name whosoever believeth in him shall receive remission of sins*” (Acts 10:43).

Verily these are words whereby you may be saved. The Son of God came here, suffered, died, rose, that such words might be sounded in your ears, and that believing in Him, you might have remission of sins through His Name. Then take God at His word at this moment. Your sins are great and many, your unworthiness beyond description, but, notwithstanding all, you may be saved. Your need and ruin could only be met by a divine Saviour: remission of sins could only come to you by the shedding of His blood. But everything that was needed has been provided by God; redemption’s mighty work has been accomplished by the Son of His love; and through faith in Him you may have the knowledge of salvation by the remission of your sins. What a glorious message! How worthy of the God of all grace who sends it forth! How worthy of the universal and whole-hearted acceptation of the sinners to whom it comes!

There is one solemn verse of Peter's address which I have passed over. Here it is -

"*And he commanded us to preach unto the people, and to testify that it is he which was ordained of God to be the judge of quick and dead*" (Acts 10:42).

Note this well! The One whose name is now proclaimed as Saviour will one day be the "Judge of quick and dead". If you do not know Him as Saviour you will have to know Him as Judge. How will you meet Him whose Name and work you have despised, and whose words of love you have disregarded? Ah! when that dread moment comes how much would you give to have again the golden opportunity of this hour of grace! But it will then be too late! Alas for the procrastinators and the almost persuaded ones in that day! Alas for the unbelievers in that day! Then do not throw your soul away in the folly of unbelief. "Today, if ye will hear his voice, harden not your heart". God is speaking today in words whereby you may be saved. Take good heed to those words, I beseech you. Discredit all human testimony if you will; be a sceptic in history, in biography, in science, but do not plunge your soul into the guilty darkness which must enshroud the one *who makes God a liar.* Do not quench the only light whose kindly ray, like Bethlehem's star, can lead you to a Saviour.

"If we receive the witness of men, the witness

of God is greater; for this is the witness of God which he hath testified of his Son. He that believeth on the Son of God hath the witness in himself; he that believeth not God hath made him a liar; because he believeth not the record that God gave of his Son" (1 John 5:9-10).

PAUL'S COMMISSION

The Lord Jesus Christ in heavenly glory sent His servant Paul to "open their eyes, and to turn them from darkness to light, and from the power of Satan unto God, that they may receive forgiveness of sins, and inheritance among them which are sanctified by faith that is in me" (Acts 26:18).

The first item in the commission is to "open their eyes". This brings before us the plain fact that none are convicted of sin except by the grace of God. It is not *natural* for any of us to be brought to a sense of our true condition before God; it is as great a miracle as the raising of a dead man when a child of Adam begins to feel the burden of sin. When a man comes into anxiety about the need of his soul it is a great miracle - it is the finger of God.

Those whose eyes are opened really know that they are sinners before God. Many will say, "We are all sinners"; they have been taught to say so, and there is enough Christian light abroad to make people willing to admit in word that they are sinners. But it is not a reality to them; they are not a bit troubled about it. If you tell a man that his house is on fire, it makes a great impression on him; it is too serious a matter to trifle with. If his children are stricken down with some deadly disease, he will spend his last penny to get the best advice and the most suitable things for them. If he finds that his money is in a bank that is not trustworthy, he will not leave it there. But when it is a question of his soul, and of the affairs of eternity, he will admit that his condition is bad and his peril great, and yet he is not sufficiently concerned even to take the matter into serious consideration.

The man of the world says: "The subject of religion is one on which there is great difference of opinion, and we do not really know what to believe; we have serious intellectual difficulties as to believing anything at all". But this matter has nothing whatever to do with the intellect; it is purely an affair of the conscience. Do you want more evidence to convince you that you are *a sinner*? Do you want stronger proof that you are *not right with God*? Let the still small voice of conscience speak in the secret chambers of your soul.

It is not a question of your mind being convinced by an intellectual process, but of your giving in to God and taking your true place before Him. Job had intellectual difficulties for a long time. If you want to see a masterpiece of philosophical argument read the book of Job. Job and his three friends discussed these matters until the Lord came in and asserted His place in Job's conscience; then the discussion was silenced, and the intellectual difficulties vanished like shadows of the night before the sun. Then Job cried, "Mine eye seeth thee, wherefore I abhor myself, and repent in dust and ashes". If you get into the dust and ashes of self-judgment your soul will get blessing from God.

The next item in the commission is "to turn them from darkness to light". It is not enough that men should find out they are sinners; they must also be shown God's way of salvation; for when the eyes of sinners are opened they often say: "I must reform my life, I must change my habits; I must sign the pledge; I must join the church; I must take up some good work; I must give something to religious causes", and so on. They think that by this they will get into God's favour, and that their sins will be blotted out. All this is *darkness*, because such things as these have no efficacy to cleanse from sin - they do not bring salvation. You must have the salvation question settled before you begin to think about serving God. You may change your manner of life by an act of your own will. A piece of lead might be made to look like a five-shilling piece. It might be a perfect imitation, but it would be of no value. That is like a mere outward change of life. It will not do. Salvation is a divine work; it is of the Lord; and without the salvation of God you will perish.

Salvation has been secured by the precious atoning work of the Son of God. There will be multitudes in glory that no man can number, and if they were asked how they got there, each one would point to the Lamb in the *midst* of the throne, and say, "He did it". He bore the judgment of God and went into death, and He is now in resurrection-triumph at the right hand of God. The very fact that He is seated on the throne of God proclaims the value of His work, and if you rest on that work it will secure to you a purged conscience. May Jesus' precious work be the present and eternal resting place of your soul!

But another says: "It is not works that I wish to have, but I want to be sure that the Spirit of God has really wrought in my soul; I want to feel the evidences of His working in my heart". In this case the darkness is all the more subtle because there is an element of truth connected with it. It is true that there must be a work of the Spirit of God in the soul, and indeed without His work none would ever be convicted of sin. But the first work of the Spirit is rather to make you feel that you are utterly unfit for God and deserving of hell. This is the Spirit's work when He awakens a sinner, and if you are convinced of this, it is the best evidence that the Spirit has wrought in you. Spiritual experiences and emotions are very blessed, but they are not the foundation of faith. People are often deceived by their feelings and experiences, and Satan can go a long way in imitating these things. It is something outside ourselves which brings assurance, even the Word of God. Innumerable scriptures assure the believer of eternal safety and blessing, and these scriptures are unchanging. Whether you are groaning in the valley or singing on the mount with God, His Word remains unchanged. It was the key of promise that opened the dungeon of Doubting Castle; but, thank God, we have something even better than *promises*. If God had given us promises, I trust we should not have doubted Him, but He has given us more. Christ Jesus came into the world to save sinners, and died upon the cross to put away the sins of all who believe on His name. God has raised Him from the dead, and set Him at His own right hand in heavenly glory. These things are not promises, they are accomplished facts. Before Christ came it was a time of promises, but the gospel today is a proclamation of facts.

There is another form of darkness which troubles many. They are not sure that theirs is the *right kind* of faith. Such persons are unconsciously making a saviour of their faith - taking the crown from the brow of Jesus and putting it on their faith. The wrong kind of faith is faith which rests in a wrong object. If your faith is in the Lord Jesus Christ it is the right kind of faith. Faith is the eye that looks at Jesus, and the fact that you see beauty and attractiveness in Him is the proof that you have faith. Then turn from the darkness into the light. What glorious light! Light shining in a Saviour's face! May that glory shine upon you even now!

"From the power of Satan unto God". Many souls have really been convicted of sin, and have bowed in secret before God with desire to be saved, but they have not got the blessing because there is something from which they cannot break away. Something of the world holds them. They are not prepared to turn from the things which keep them from Christ and from God. It may be worldly friends, or some form of pleasure; it may be reading, music, drink, gambling - a thousand different things in a thousand different cases; but whatever it is that thus keeps the soul from turning to God, it is "the power of Satan". The prodigal had to arise and go to the father; he had to turn from the far country and the husks. There is a decisive moment when, by God's grace, the sinner turns to Him; the misery and pressure of sin become greater than the pleasure it affords, and the goodness and grace of God are so known that the soul turns to Him. This causes joy in the presence of the angels of God, for it is really the recovery of the lost sinner, and shows that God has, in some measure at least, got His right place in the sinner's conscience, and in the confidence of the sinner's heart. It sets God free to bestow on him all the blessings of divine love and grace. The moment you really turn to God, your reception and the blessings you receive must be measured altogether by what is in the heart of God.

"That they may receive forgiveness of sins, and inheritance among them which are sanctified by faith that is in me". It is a great thing when we give God His right place, and are prepared to *receive* from Him - prepared to be needy and helpless sinners, and to take in simple faith His priceless gifts.

Another scripture declares that "through this man is preached unto you forgiveness of sins: and by him all that believe are justified from all things" (Acts 13:38, 39). Nothing could be plainer. Will you believe this good news, and receive the pardon of which it speaks? Those who receive the forgiveness of sins also receive a heavenly "inheritance:"

You must either inherit with Christ or with the devil. There is a place prepared for the devil and his angels, and those who do not receive forgiveness of sins will inherit with him. Believers will be with Christ and like Him for ever; they will inherit with Christ. Thus they can truly sing

"With Him we love in spotless white,
In glory we shall shine,
His blissful presence our delight,
In love and joy divine".
"All taint of sin shall be removed,
All evil done away,
And we shall dwell with God's Beloved,
Through God's eternal day".

JACOB'S DREAM

When Jacob "went out from Beersheba, and went toward Haran" (Genesis 28:10), he was fleeing from the consequences of his sins as recorded in the previous chapter. The prophet Hosea says, "Jacob *fled* into the country of Syria" (12:12). He was leaving Beersheba, which means "the well of the oath" - a place of refreshment and satisfaction - and was going toward Haran, which means "a parched, dry place". He represents a sinner, afraid of the consequences of his sins, but turning to the world for comfort and satisfaction instead of to God.

In the course of his journey "he lighted upon a certain place, and tarried there all night, because the sun was set; and he took of the stones of that place, and put them for his pillow, and lay down in that place to sleep" (Genesis 28:11). In this sleeping man can be seen a true picture of the state in which thousands are found today. They have sinned; their faces are towards the world; but, with unbelief for a pillow, they are in a profound slumber of spiritual indifference. But as God came in to awaken Jacob, so He still comes in to awaken the slumbering consciences of men.

is when he is made conscious of the reality of divine and eternal things. Many have been spiritually awakened - like Jacob - by a dream. John Bunyan was awakened by a dream that he was just dropping into the flames of hell when a Person in white raiment suddenly plucked him as a brand out of the fire. George Whitefield was awakened when a schoolboy sixteen years of age by a dream that he saw God on Mount Sinai. And many others have been "warned of God" in dreams.

Are we, then, to set aside spiritual concern until some terror-striking vision haunts our midnight hours? Certainly not; for we must ever remember that, though God is pleased to use oftentimes such things as dreams, sicknesses, providential mercies, and calamities to awaken sinners, His great approach to man is by

THE GOSPEL OF HIS GRACE.

Nothing could be more calculated to arrest a sinner's conscience, or to bring spiritual concern into his heart, than the gospel. It exposes his need by setting forth the greatness of the grace which alone could meet that need. It brings the righteousness of God into view; it presents a Person with whom every man must have to do, either as Saviour or Judge; it deals with questions of the utmost moment, in which every man, woman, and child has a personal interest, the issues of which will fill eternity. In short, the gospel leaves everyone who hears it absolutely without excuse, for it presents everything that is calculated to open men's eyes, and to turn them from darkness to light.

Without attempting to *interpret* Jacob's dream - which, I believe, has special reference to the blessing of God's earthly people Israel - I think we may see in it three things which are eminently characteristic of the gospel: (1) God was revealed in grace; (2) heaven was brought into view and put in communication with earth; and (3) man was found in a place which was "none other but the house of God" and "the gate of heaven".

1. *God revealed in grace.* "The land whereon thou liest, to thee will I give it ... and in thee and in thy seed shall all the families of the earth be blessed. And, behold, I am with thee, and will keep thee in all places whither thou goest, and will bring thee again into this land; for I will not leave thee, until I have done that which I have spoken to thee of".

God revealed Himself as One who would *give*, and *bless*, and *keep*; and all this is absolute *grace*, for certainly there was nothing in Jacob to merit such favour.

It is thus that God declares Himself in the gospel of His grace. Everything is in perfect contrast to the principle of the law. A divine *claim* upon man for moral perfection could only expose the fact that man is a moral bankrupt, and has "nothing to pay". Thus "by the law is the knowledge of sin". But according to grace we have to do with a giving God. "God so loved the world that he gave his only begotten Son" (John 3:16). God has provided infinite blessing for man in absolute grace, and puts it all within the reach of man as a gift. "The scripture hath concluded all under sin, that the promise by faith of Jesus Christ might be given to them that believe" (Galatians 3:22). "I will give unto him that is athirst of the fountain of the water of life freely" (Revelation 21:6). Hence on our side it is not a question of doing or paying, but of receiving. "That they may receive forgiveness of sins" (Acts 26:18). "Through his name whosoever believeth in him shall receive remission of sins" (Acts 10:43). "That we might receive the promise of the Spirit through faith" (Galatians 3:14); "That we might receive the adoption of sons" (Galatians 4:5).

How suitable is this! and how worthy of God! If man is altogether worthless and lost, blessing can only come to him as a gift; but in being presented as a gift it is made available for all. And if we receive by faith blessings which are wholly of God we have complete assurance of the divine perfection and stability of all that we receive. Every blessing has been brought by the Son of God, has been secured in righteousness by His death, and is established in Him as the risen and glorified One.

Then if God *gives* and *blesses*, He also *keeps*. The perfect and eternal security of the believer is in God. "I will not leave thee", was His word to Jacob, "until I have done that which I have spoken to thee of". Believers are *kept* by God's power, through faith. God will never leave nor forsake His saints. Having begun a good work in them He will not fail to complete it until the day of Jesus Christ. How perfect is this grace which the gospel reveals!

2. *Heaven brought into view*. Man has forfeited his right to live upon the earth; sin has brought him under death. And it is a great principle with God that when He acts in grace He never merely restores what has been forfeited, but bestows that which is higher and greater than the thing forfeited. The thief on the cross was not restored to honour and dignity in the place where his life was forfeited, but he got something infinitely higher in being taken with Jesus into paradise.

The gospel brings light *from heaven*, for it presents a Saviour glorified at the right hand of God. The grace and glory of God are set forth in the Lord Jesus Christ, and as He is preached "with the Holy Ghost *sent down from heaven*", heaven is put into communication with earth. It is not now *angels* ascending and descending - figurative of the providential care of heaven - but the Holy Spirit come down from a glorified Saviour to testify the gospel of the grace of God.

3. *The house of God and the gate of heaven.* The end which God has in view in the gospel is that men should be brought into His house. We see this in the parable of the great supper (Luke 14), which shows that God will have men to be brought into the circle of His own satisfaction. Everything contrary to God's pleasure having been judged and removed in the death of Christ, He now finds His eternal rest and satisfaction in that blessed One, and in His infinite grace He would have men brought into that satisfaction. Thus the great supper is a scene of heavenly festivity. Its joys are tasted here by the Spirit, but they are heavenly joys, and the house of God may fitly be called "the gate of heaven".

Jacob's response to this wondrous revelation of grace and glory was very poor. And in this respect he is a true representative of many who hear the gospel. "He was afraid" of the *glory*, as well he might be; and to the *grace* he only responded with a miserable "if". How many are like this! They have the fear of God before them in a certain way, but are on a legal, bargain-making line. The barbed arrows of divine conviction stick fast in their consciences; but they are not prepared to receive grace or to break with the world. They try to compromise the matter and to secure favour from God by a measure of religious earnestness and devotedness. Some will literally, like Jacob, give a tenth to God, and many are practically on that line. They make a kind of religious bargain with God. This is a very different thing from simply receiving His grace, and practically, as we see in Jacob's case, it does not separate them from the world.

Jacob went on his way into Mesopotamia - the country out of which Abraham had been called - and lived there twenty years. He got married, prospered in business, and was, as the world would say, a successful man. But I do not think he ever forgot Bethel. Outwardly prosperous as he was, his own inner experience was not very bright. "Thus I was; in the day the drought consumed me, and the frost by night; and my sleep departed from mine eyes. Thus have I been twenty years in thy house; I served thee fourteen years for thy two daughters, and six years for thy cattle: and thou hast changed my wages ten times" (Genesis 31:40-41).

Here we see, in figure, an awakened sinner seeking rest and satisfaction in the world, but finding that all its varied store fails to give peace to the conscience or joy to the heart. Many a man seems to begetting on well in the world, but if you could look into his heart you would find it full of unrest and disappointment. God's arrow of conviction is in his soul, and he cannot find what he wants in the world. It took twenty years of labour and disappointment to make Jacob willing to leave the "far country". Often a long time elapses between the sinner's first *awakening* and his conversion - that is, his definite turning to God.

At the end of twenty years God spoke to Jacob, saying, "I am the God of Bethel, where thou anointedst the pillar, and where thou vowedst a vow unto me: now arise, get thee out from this land, and return unto the land of thy kindred" (Genesis 31:13). What a history had come in between the "where" and the "now"! What afflictions, exercises, and disappointments had been needed to prepare Jacob for the call to "Arise"! And has it not been so with ourselves? Have not some of us had to prove through long years of experience the emptiness of the world? We have had to be brought to cry, like the prodigal, "I perish with hunger". Our souls, as divinely awakened, could not rest in anything but the knowledge of God, and that we could not find in the world.

"Now *arise*", is the call of God to every awakened sinner. "I will arise and go unto my father", says the repentant prodigal. The soul - sick of sin and of the world - arises to turn to God as the living source of all good and blessing. This is conversion. God's grace is ever toward men, but how slow are men to turn to God for the blessings of His grace! Did they but know the riches and glory of God's grace, and the festivity of heaven over one repenting sinner, not all the splendid trifles of earth could hold them at a distance from God. Beloved friends, infinite grace waits to welcome you, and to enrich you. Will you not "repent and turn to God"? (Acts 26:20). Oh! Now, arise and return!

"Jacob rose up, and set his sons and his wives upon camels; and he carried away all his cattle, and all his goods ... to go to Isaac his father in the land of Canaan" (Geneasis 31:17-18). This was a move in the right direction, but he had yet to learn that all his own resources and strength were of no avail, and that his deliverance and blessing must be

ENTIRELY OF GOD.

He was brought to this point by the experiences recorded in Genesis 32.

"And the messengers returned to Jacob, saying, We came to thy brother Esau, and also he cometh to meet thee, and four hundred men with him. Then Jacob was greatly afraid and distressed" (Genesis 32:6-7). He was now brought face to face with the sins of the past. The whole question from which he had escaped for twenty years was now re-opened. And so it is with the awakened sinner. A moment comes when questions have to be thoroughly bottomed, when there can be no evasion or compromise. The sinner must learn his own utter inability, he must be stripped of all his resources, he must find himself "alone" and helpless, he must be altogether cast upon God. This is the lesson Jacob had to learn in Genesis 32.

He divides his property, and sends drove

after drove as a present to "appease" Esau. It was no question of a tenth, or even of nine-tenths, now. He sent over "all that he had", and "was left alone" (Genesis 32:23-24). Was he satisfied? Could all these resources and presents secure him? Not at all. Ah! sinners have to learn that all their resources are worthless to secure blessing. All that you have done, are doing, or will ever be able to do, is of no account whatever in this matter. You must have to do with God alone, as a sinner, *and nothing but a sinner.*

And not only have we to learn that our resources fail, but every kind of self-reliance has to be broken down. Believers have often a large measure of unbroken self-confidence, and it hinders them from knowing the full blessedness of the salvation of God. Sooner or later God will discover it, and break it. "There wrestled a man" with Jacob, "and when he saw that he prevailed not against him, he touched the hollow of his thigh; and the hollow of Jacob's thigh was out of joint, as he wrestled with him" (Genesis 32:24-25).

Wrestling Jacob did *not* get the blessing. It was when he could wrestle no longer - for his wrestling was the resistance of an unsubdued will - that "He blessed him there". So long as self-confidence in any shape or form is found with us we wrestle, and are really in conflict with God. But when God gets us alone with Himself He puts His finger on the place where our strength lies, and reduces us to conscious helplessness. Then we learn the true blessedness of faith. Faith *clings*, and clings only to God.

"I will not let thee go, except thou bless me", is the language not of one who *wrestles*, but of one who *clings*. His earthly resources all gone, his strength reduced to helplessness, he could only *cling*. And "He blessed him there". God loves to be known and trusted - He loves to be taken hold of by the faith of sinners, as a Saviour God. All that He is in this wondrous character, He is for sinners who are absolutely without righteousness or strength, and the faith that clings to Him secures the blessing. "Abraham believed God, and it was counted to him for righteousness ... Now it was not written for his sake alone, that it was imputed to him: but for us also to whom it shall be imputed, if we believe on him that raised up Jesus our Lord from the dead; who was delivered for our offences, and was raised again for our justification". "To him that worketh not, but believeth on him that justifieth the ungodly, his faith is counted for righteousness" (Romans 4).

May each awakened sinner be brought to this blessed faith in a Saviour God!

SAMSON'S RIDDLE

*"Out of the eater came forth meat, and out of the strong came forth sweetness".*Judges 14:14

The riddle which Samson put forth to his guests, and which they could not expound, is very suggestive of the truth of the gospel. And the incident upon which it was founded is a striking picture of what has been accomplished by the Lord Jesus.

Samson was on the way to secure the object of his affections, when "a young lion roared against him, and the Spirit of the Lord came mightily upon him, and he rent him as he would have rent a kid, and he had nothing in his hand". Then on a subsequent occasion "he turned aside to see the carcase of the lion; and, behold, there was a swarm of bees and honey in the carcase of the lion". This circumstance gave rise to the riddle which so puzzled Samson's guests, and we may bc sure that God gave it a place in Scripture as being figurative of Christ's great victory and its infinite results in blessing.

The Son of God has come forth into this world to secure blessing for man, and to bring men into the circle of divine love, but on His way to accomplish this He had to meet and overcome the power of death. This was absolutely necessary, because all those whose blessing was in view were under the sentence and power of death. Whatever may be your position in society, or however excellent your conduct as a man amongst men, you are under the sentence of death. Nor is death a merely natural event which follows upon the operation of certain natural processes of disease and decay. Men would like to regard it as being only this, but Scripture makes it very clear that death is the wages of sin, the power of Satan, and the judgment of God.

When you committed your first sin you forfeited your title to live upon the earth, and but for God's mercy you would have died that moment. Death has "passed upon all men, for that all have sinned" (Romans 5). Death is no part of the course of nature as God constituted it, it is "the wages of sin".

Then we read in Scripture of "him that had the power of death, that is, the devil" (Hebrews 2:14). By reason of the fall, and in consequence of sin, the devil has acquired power over man. The devil sought to accomplish man's destruction from the place in which God set him as in favour and blessing on the earth, and having succeeded in bringing man under sin he has so far gained his point. The truth and righteousness of God necessitate that the pronounced sentence should be executed. And thus the devil has a claim, if we may so say, upon man, he has acquired a right to demand that death should come upon man. Satan, in this sense, wields the power of death. Man's sin has invested him with the right to claim the execution of the sentence of death upon man.

It thus appears most clearly that death is not, as people say, the "debt of nature". It is the solemn judgment of God upon a fallen creature - a judgment which cannot be reversed or modified in any way.

Not one of Adam's race can escape the devouring fury of this great "eater", or can resist the desolating power of this "strong" enemy. It is said of the lion that "he turneth not aside for any"; and this is true of death. Prince, peer, and peasant alike fall before him. What are high-sounding titles, the applause of multitudes, millions of gold, or all the coveted prizes of ambition or selfishness in the presence of death? At the gates of death the monarch, the millionaire, and the mendicant meet on a common level. All are alike fallen and lost. Each finds himself stripped of everything that he acquired or possessed here - stripped of all save a creature's responsibility and the guilt of unnumbered sins.

Do you not, then, fear death? Is it not a terrible enemy in your eyes? I trust that, to some extent at least, the fear of death is before your soul. For, if so, you can hardly be indifferent to the blessed facts foreshadowed in Samson's victory and its consequences. And Samson's riddle may become pregnant with divine light and blessing for your soul. May God grant it in His great mercy!

God has brought meat out of the eater, and sweetness out of the strong. He has laid help upon One who is mighty. The Son of His love has come forth to meet and overthrow the power of death and has triumphed gloriously. His be the victor's name!

But before I speak of how the power of death has been broken, I would fain occupy your heart with the glories and perfections of the Person who has undertaken and accomplished this mighty work. I would have you to know how capable and how suitable He was to bear the brunt of this great conflict. I have already dwelt upon the terribleness of death as the wages of sin, the power of Satan, and the judgment of God. Now it must be clear to everyone that no person could undertake to deliver others from a power to which he himself was subject. The first requisite in a Saviour is that He must be personally exempt from sin, free from Satan's power, and in no wise subject to the judgment of God. It would be impossible for one to come under these things on behalf of others if he was under them on his own account. Hence the sacrifices must be without blemish, or they would have presented no fitting type of the true victim.

Three precious statements of Scripture will bring before us the moral qualification of the Lord Jesus to go into death on behalf of others.

1. "That holy thing which shall be born of thee shall be called the Son of God". Such were Gabriel's words to the blessed virgin when he announced the advent of the Son of the Highest. It would be impossible for a divine Being ever to be personally tainted with sin. If God comes here in flesh it must be holy flesh. Hence the Spirit of God can not only say "He did no sin", but that He "knew no sin". Sin was as far removed from Him morally as the depths of hell are distant from the courts of glory. So that death as the wages of sin could never have touched Him.

2. "The prince of this world cometh, and hath nothing in me" (John 14:30). That these words had special force at the moment when they were uttered I doubt not, but they express what was ever true of that blessed One. He was ever beyond the range of Satan's influence, ever invulnerable and invincible in presence of all Satan's fiery darts. There was at last a Man here upon whom Satan could fasten no claim. Do you think the devil could ever have claimed that He should die? Never! The Prince of life owes no tribute to the prince of this world, so that death, as the power of Satan, could never have touched Him.

3. “This is my beloved Son” (Luke 9:35). Here we have expressed from “the excellent glory”, as Peter calls it, God’s estimate of Him. Romans 3 tells us that all the world has become “subject to the judgment of God”; but here is a Man who is radiant with every moral perfection and is the object of the Father’s delight and love. What has death as the judgment of God to say to Him? Nothing! Absolutely nothing. The glory saluted Him and embraced Him. “He received from God the Father honour and glory”. Thus we behold Him, personally exempt from death in every aspect.

Now I trust you are somewhat prepared to appreciate the transcendent grace in which He has come under death on behalf of others. He came “to give his life a ransom for many” (Mark 10:45). No one could righteously *give* something which was already forfeited. But He could *give* in boundless grace His holy life “a ransom for many”. Grace brought that blessed One to the place where sin brought us. “The wages of sin” have been paid to One who received them as having come in infinite grace into the place of the sinner. “While we were yet sinners, Christ died for us”.

Thus the devil is annulled, as having “the power of death”. When the devil so far triumphed as to bring man by sin under the righteous sentence of death, he could never have thought that the One who pronounced the sentence would bear it Himself. He could never have imagined that One personally exempt from it would come under it in love. He could never have anticipated that death's dark vale would be lighted up with the love of God, and made the way of life for man. No! such thoughts as these could only have their birth in the mind of infinite love.

The full weight of God's holy judgment upon a fallen and guilty creature has been borne by Him who came under it in absolute personal perfection according to the will of God. God "made him to be sin for us, who knew no sin; that we might be made the righteousness of God in him" (2 Corinthians 5:21).

"Our Saviour Jesus Christ ... hath abolished death, and hath brought life and incorruptibility to light through the gospel" (2 Timothy 1:10). The shadows of death have rolled for ever from His brow, and life and incorruptibility are seen in Him. And He is not only out of death Himself, but He has power to let others out - He has "the keys of hell and of death". If you fall down at His feet He will put the right hand of His power upon you, and say, "Fear not" (Revelation 1:17, 18). How good to know that He has died so that He might have in resurrection the unchallenged power of life and blessing towards those who were under death.

Thus, by the grace and love of God, the "eater" has been caused to yield "meat", and out of the "strong" has come "sweetness". On the ground of the death of Christ all man's necessities as a sinner before God can be met. He may have forgiveness of sins, justification, peace with God, deliverance from the fear of death, salvation from all the power of evil, and grace for support in weakness and trial. All these blessings, and much more, are secured by the death of Christ, and may be received through faith in Him.

But there is "sweetness" as well as "meat"! Grace has luxuries to bestow as well as necessaries. The gospel not only meets all man's need, but it brings to him a wonderful *excess* of blessing. The death of Christ becomes to the believer's heart the blessed witness of the love of God. We perceive love in that "he laid down his life for us" (1 John 3:16). God would have us to appropriate the "sweetness" of His own love expressed in the death of Christ. He has given His Spirit to shed this love abroad in our hearts, and to form us in response to it.

Sin and death seemed to shut out man from God, and God from man, but by the death of Christ all that excluded man from God has been judged and removed, and at the same time God has been fully revealed to man.

One closing word of appeal. The Person and work of Christ have once more been presented to you. But with what result? Hearing of Christ can only add to your condemnation if you do not receive Him by faith as your

Saviour. You cannot say that He is unworthy of your trust. Nor can you afford to do without Him. *Without Christ* nothing lies before you but death and judgment, and at any moment your doom may be sealed for ever. Then believe on Him now, and receive the "abundance of grace" which God is freely giving through Him.

THE KING AND THE CRIPPLE

2 Samuel 9

The incidents of this chapter present a lovely picture of the grace of God to sinful men. David, after years of wandering and warfare, was at last securely seated on the throne of Israel. With prosperity at home and peace abroad the king's generous heart sought an object on which to bestow his royal bounty, and hence the gracious inquiry with which the chapter opens, "Is there any that is left of the house of Saul, that I may shew him kindness?"

Saul had sought to pierce David with a javelin even to the wall. Again and again he had attempted to lay violent hands on David, and had pursued him upon the mountains like a partridge. He had, moreover, hated him without a cause. Yet when David was established on his throne he said, "Is there yet any that is left of *the house of Saul*, that I may shew him kindness?" and again in verse 3, "Is there not yet any of the house of Saul, that I may shew the kindness of God unto him?"

The kindness of God goes out to His enemies and to the utterly undeserving. Otherwise it would never reach lost and guilty men. "For we ourselves also were sometimes foolish, disobedient, deceived, serving divers lusts and pleasures, living in malice and envy, hateful, and hating one another. But after that the kindness and love of God our Saviour toward man appeared, not by works of righteousness which we have done, but according to his mercy he saved us" (Titus 3:3-5).

A wicked girl, in a frenzy of passion, struck her Christian mother with the poker, crying, "I would kill your God if I could get at Him". The kindness of God is toward such a one as that. You may be shocked at such bold wickedness, but remember that a deceitful and desperately wicked heart beats within your own breast. Have you never had hard and rebellious thoughts of God? It is true of all, that "the carnal mind is *enmity against God*: for it is not subject to the law of God, neither indeed can be. So then they that are in the flesh cannot please God" (Romans 8:7, 8).

Man's enmity against God was proved at the cross. God was in Christ reconciling the world unto Himself, but it would not be reconciled. God presented His grace to a guilty world, but the world's answer was the rejection and murder of His beloved Son. But, in spite of this, God's attitude towards men is one of "kindness and pity". For well-nigh two thousand years He has continued to proclaim by His servants "repentance and remission of sins" in the name of the Lord Jesus "among all nations". This is

His attitude towards men is one of infinite grace, and He desires that His grace should be known even by those who have said in their hearts, if not with their lips, "Depart from us, for we desire not the knowledge of thy ways".

"And Ziba said unto the king, Jonathan hath yet a son, which is lame on his feet". In chapter 4 we are told how Mephibosheth became a cripple. "He was five years old when the tidings came of Saul and Jonathan out of Jezreel, and his nurse took him up, and fled: and it came to pass, as she made haste to flee, that he fell, and became lame". The present condition of man is figuratively set before us in this *fallen cripple.*

When God created Adam and Eve, He put them in a place prepared by His own hands for their reception. Everything in the garden of Eden ("pleasantness") witnessed to the goodness of God. The fruitful tree, the flowing rivers, the golden sunlight, all declared with harmonious voice that God was good. But man had not been made as a mere machine, or as an irresponsible animal. He was an intelligent and responsible moral being, and to remind him of this, as well as to test his obedience, he was forbidden to eat of the tree of the knowledge of good and evil. The penalty of death was attached to disobedience.

While Adam and Eve obeyed the command of

God they were innocent and happy. But the serpent came upon the scene and suggested that God was not good, and that He was keeping back from man something that would be for man's benefit to possess. Losing confidence in God, and carried away by lust and pride, our first parents fell from their happy state of innocence, and came not only under the power of sin and Satan, but also under the penalty of death.

Thus, in the very infancy of the race, man fell and became a moral cripple; he cannot walk with God; he cannot run in the way of God's commandments; he has fallen and become lame on his feet. And, like Mephibosheth, he is lame on *both* his feet. He is defective and incapable in his responsibilities both towards God and his neighbour.

People do not like to admit that they are entirely crippled. They do not mind confessing in a general way that they do not walk quite straight. They will say, "We are all sinners; we all have our shortcomings, etc.", and many try to remedy their defects by resolutions, vows, pledges, turning new leaves, and other crutches and appliances of similar nature. But human efforts are in vain. It remains ever true that man is "without strength" (Romans 5:6); he is destitute of power to perform the will of God. How good it is to know that God in grace does not claim from man that which cannot be rendered, but that "To him that worketh not, but believeth on him that justifieth the ungodly, his faith is counted for righteousness"! (Romans 4:5).

"And the king said unto him, Where is he? And Ziba said unto the king, Behold, he is in the house of Machir, the son of Ammiel, in Lo-debar".

The sinner's *condition* we have already dwelt upon, and now we come to his *position.* Lo-debar means a place of no pasture, and it fitly represents the world. It may seem strange to speak of the world as a place of no pasture, for its things are very attractive to the natural man. The world's things are perfectly adapted to suit the tastes, and gratify the desires, of man as a fallen sinner. But, viewed morally, the world is a desert, because the knowledge of God cannot be found there. The world is a vast system of things in which men seek to make themselves as happy as possible *at a distance from God.* Thus, in a true and divine sense, the world is a veritable Lo-debar. It contains nothing to minister to the deepest necessities of man; for of what avail are all its boasted stores of wisdom, honour, wealth, end pleasure, if God remains unknown? Sad is the portion of those who are "without God in the world" (Ephesians 2:12), for they are strangers to that in which alone true satisfaction can be found by human hearts!

"And king David sent, and fetched him out of

the house of Machir, the son of Ammiel, from Lo-debar".

Here we see, in figure, the activity of God's grace. If the sinner cannot remedy his own imperfections, and if he is at a distance from God without desire to seek after God, blessing must come in altogether from God's side. In the gospel of His grace God approaches men as they are and where they are, and makes Himself known as a Saviour God. It is by the gospel that God brings men to a knowledge of Himself. Then it is of all importance that we should know the true nature of the gospel of God.

Briefly stated, the gospel is (1) the presentation of a Person; (2) the declaration of what that Person has undergone, and of God's actings towards Him; and (3) the proclamation of repentance and remission of sins in His Name.

1. The Person whom the gospel presents is the Son of God. By sending His Son into the world God presented Himself in grace to men. There was no form of human need that He was not able and willing to meet; there was no kind of pressure upon man that He could not relieve. He "went about doing good, and healing all that were oppressed of the devil: for God was with him" (Acts 10:38). He came not to condemn the world, not to impute trespasses to men, but to present in the excellence of His

own Person the all-blessing grace of God.

There was also in Him the complete setting forth of everything that was according to God's good pleasure in a Man. He was the beloved Son, in whom the Father was well pleased. Every divine perfection was brought near to men in pure grace in that blessed and holy Person. And every one whose heart was attracted by His grace, and believed on Him, obtained forgiveness of sins and found the knowledge of God.

2. But this wondrous grace must reign *through righteousness*, and it could only be presented to men in One who was willing and competent to charge Himself with the liabilities of men. The Lord Jesus could speak of forgiveness of sins because He was about to bear sins in His own body on the tree; He could heal every disease, and rescue men from the power of death itself because He had come in grace to undergo all that was due to men in consequence of sin. In the days of His flesh the accomplishment of all this was future, but it is now past, and the gospel declares what He has undergone on man's behalf. He has borne and suffered for sins, has been made sin, and has tasted death. He charged Himself with the liabilities of men, and has undergone the holy judgment due to sin. And all this in absolute grace, that the grace of God might flow out in righteousness to men.

Then the gospel declares further how God has acted towards the One who thus came in grace into man's condemnation. God raised Him from the dead, so that He saw no corruption, and He lives for evermore beyond the reach of sin and death. Man, in the Person of the Lord Jesus, has an entirely new place with God, and is found in a state to which no imperfection or condemnation can ever attach. Nothing has been overlooked or compromised. Sins have been borne, sin has been judged, death has been suffered, Satan's power overthrown, and all this by One who is now raised from the dead as the glorious witness to the complete triumph of grace.

3. Now we get the proclamation of forgiveness of sins. "Be it known unto you therefore, men and brethren, that through this man is preached unto you the forgiveness of sins: and by him, all that believe are justified from all things, from which ye could not be justified by the law of Moses" (Acts 13:38, 39). God thus approaches men in unmingled grace, as One who "will have all men to be saved". He is made known through the Lord Jesus Christ as a Justifier and a Saviour God. He sets forth what He is that He may be known and believed on in that character. And "all that believe are justified from all things". If we believe on Him that raised up Jesus our Lord from the dead, righteousness is imputed to us. And "being justified by faith, we have peace with God

through our Lord Jesus Christ".

It is by this wondrous and blessed gospel that God approaches man in his ruin and distance. This gospel, received by faith, gives man the knowledge of God in grace, and brings him away from the world where God is unknown. He leaves Lo-debar for the courts of royal grace.

How blessed to know that *the kindness of God* is toward men because of what Christ is, and on the ground of what He has accomplished! It has no respect to merit, or worthiness of any kind, in the sinner. David's kindness to Mephibosheth was according to the worthiness of another. "That I may shew him kindness *for Jonathan's sake*", and "I will surely shew thee kindness *for Jonathan thy father's sake*". The excellence and perfection of Christ are now before God, and all His grace to men is according to His estimation of Christ. Can anyone say that such infinite grace as this is not "worthy of all acceptation"? Then why not believe, and receive it *now*?

Another thought we may gather from the picture before us is that the known grace of God not only separates a man from the world of the ungodly, but it gives him a true judgment of himself. In the presence of David's grace Mephibosheth could only say, "What is thy servant, that thou shouldest look upon such a dead dog as I am?" This is repentance - the judgment which a sinner has of himself in the presence of divine grace. “Repentance and remission of sins” are both preached in the Name of a risen Saviour.

Finally, we see here in picture the purpose which God has in view in making known His grace to men. “As for Mephibosheth, said the king, he shall eat at my table, as one of *the king’s sons*”. It is God’s purpose and pleasure that we should receive sonship (Galatians 4:5). This is not to meet our need, but to gratify His own heart. He is “bringing many sons to glory” (Hebrews 2: 10). The love of God will find its satisfaction in having a company “conformed to the image of his Son, that he might be the firstborn among many brethren” (Romans 8:29). And God delights that even here His children should know, by the Spirit, the liberty with which the Son makes free. Liberty to be in the *home circle* of divine affections, and to respond to those affections with the cry of sonship, “Abba, Father”. May God affect our hearts by His grace and love!

THE TWO PRODIGALS

Deuteronomy 21:18-23; Luke 15:11-24

There is a striking contrast between these two scriptures - between the prodigal who got exactly what he deserved, and the prodigal who got what he never deserved at all.

One of these two men represents each of us, for each one will either receive in righteous judgment exactly what he deserves at the hand of God, or as a penitent recipient of grace he will get blessing measured, not by his deserts, but by the love of God.

Suppose you get what you deserve, have you thought what it will be? Perhaps you suggest that God is merciful. I do not see any trace of it in the first scripture I read. "All the men of his city shall stone him with stones, that he die". If a man is to be treated as he deserves, he must not talk of mercy - it is a question of justice. Are you prepared to meet "the righteous judgment of God", and to have your deserts awarded by that holy tribunal?

God has declared that "out of the heart of men proceed evil thoughts, adulteries, fornications, murders, thefts, covetousness, wickedness, deceit, lasciviousness, an evil eye, blasphemy, pride, foolishness" (Mark 7:21-23). You may depend upon it that God knows your heart thoroughly. It is easy enough to keep up appearances before men, but God searches the heart, and knows what is there. Woe be to such a sinner, if he gets what he deserves! The eye of God searches out all the evil of your heart, and in a coming day He will judge "the secrets of men".

Every person who stands at the great white throne will get

EXACTLY WHAT HE DESERVES.

Think of the dread day in which you will be raised again to stand before God, that you may receive in holy judgment all that you deserve. Is it not a terror-striking prospect for your conscience? I know that this is a day when these things are thrust into the background, but it is a tremendous reality that there is righteous judgment with God. Take care how you brave it!

In Luke 15, we learn that all the love of God's heart is for a poor wretch who deserves

NOTHING BUT JUDGMENT.

At the end of chapter 14 the Lord told out in the plainest terms the condition of fallen men. Man created in innocence was good salt; but, alas! the salt has lost its savour, and is "neither fit for the land, nor yet for the dunghill" - fallen man is good for nothing. Having declared this, the Lord added, "He that hath ears to hear, let him hear", and we are told that "then drew near unto him all the publicans and sinners for to hear him". It was a congregation prepared to own the truth as to their good-for-nothing condition that gathered round the Lord, and heard from His lips the unfolding of this matchless grace.

The younger son was willing to take all he could get from his father, and then wanted to have nothing more to do with him. We owe our health, strength, faculties, abilities, means, and everything, that constitutes our fortune, to God; but how are we using our "portion of goods"?

Every unconverted man is afraid to trust God with his happiness; he prefers the far country to the Father's house. The thought in his mind is that he would be a loser by turning to God. What wretched pride is this! Indeed, it is the very essence of the serpent's poison first instilled into man's heart in the garden of Eden. The serpent's suggestion to Eve was, that God was withholding some good - in other words, that man could do better for himself than God was willing to do for him. The prodigal broke away in independence of will, and set up on his own account, and this is just what man has done, and each one of us in particular. "We have turned every one to his own way".

Having got away from his father, the prodigal set about to enjoy himself, and it is in one way or another, the object of every unconverted man to make himself happy; and this, regardless of the thought that he is doing so at God's expense.

Remember, you are responsible to God for every moment of a life that can only be rightly spent for His glory.

But in gratifying himself the younger son became poorer every day, and thus it is with you.

YOUR FORTUNE IS GOING FAST.

How soon you will be reduced to the poverty of a shroud! And even with all the resources of health and wealth, man gets poorer every day, because things lose their power to satisfy his heart. There was probably a moment in your history when a penny rattle would have made you perfectly happy, but a thousand pounds would not do it today. You are poorer, and you know it.

Look at Solomon with all the world's resources at his command, and yet compelled to say, "All is vanity!" A man of the world had to declare -

"My days are in the yellow leaf,
The flowers and fruits of life are gone,
The worm, the canker, and the grief
Are mine alone!" -- Lord Byron

That is what I call poverty. Queen Elizabeth reached its awful depths when she cried in her death-agony, "Millions of money for a moment of time!" There is a terrible picture of irremediable poverty in Luke 16 - poverty of the deepest kind, where a millionaire's wealth could not buy one drop of water to cool his tongue.

Thank God! if you reach the moment of poverty now, you may be eternally enriched by His wondrous grace. An old writer has said, "Free grace is a harbour that no vessel ever puts into unless driven to it".

It is a fine moment when a man comes to the end of all his resources, and must needs turn to God. "He came to himself", and the first sign of it is that he thinks of his father. "How many hired servants of my father's have bread enough to spare, and I perish with hunger!" Note those words,

"ENOUGH AND TO SPARE".

The first glimpse of light from God in our souls, is the thought that we may count upon His goodness. "I am worthless, but there is goodness in the heart of God even for a wretch like me. There is bread 'to spare', even for me".

How blessed to find that the God we have dreaded, and of whom we have thought that He wanted more from us than we could render, is waiting in infinite love for us to turn to Him for blessing! "I will arise", says the prodigal, "and go to my father, and will say unto him, Father, I have sinned against heaven, and before thee, and am no more worthy to be called thy son: make me as one of thy hired servants". Much of this is most touching and appropriate, but the last clause spoils it. It looks like humility, but in truth it is wretched pride, for it contains the assumption that he was worthy to be a hired servant. He was as little worthy to be a hired servant as he was to be a son. When people talk of hoping to be worthy of a place just inside the door, it is simply pride of heart and self-deception. If you get what you deserve it will be the lake of fire, and nothing else.

Look at this wonderful picture of grace! "When he was yet a great way off his father saw him, and had compassion, and ran, and fell on his neck, and kissed him". Footsore, heart-sick, and empty-handed he comes - his confession yet unmade - and it is enough for the father. His only qualification for favour was that he had his face turned to the father, and that was sufficient. "There is joy in the presence of the angels of God over one sinner that *repenteth*".

We hear nothing about being a hired servant after this. The father's embrace squeezed that last bit of pride out of his heart. In the presence of such grace he could only take the ground that he deserved nothing - not even to be a hired servant - and allow unmerited love to have its own wondrous way with him.

The best robe, the ring, the shoes, the fatted calf killed, and the merriment that fills the house, all express the wealth and joy of God in the riches of grace which He lavishes upon the repenting sinner. What a lovely picture! None could have told it out but the One who perfectly knew the heart of God. Do you believe that it is a true picture? Have you made this grace your own?

But is it not somewhat of a mystery that a vile and worthless sinner should have such a reception with God?

WHERE IS JUSTICE?

Where are holiness and truth? Well, be sure of this, that not one jot or tittle of the holy claims of God's majesty has had to be set aside to make way for such a result.

The closing verses of Deuteronomy 21 bring the cross before us. "And if a man have committed a sin worthy of death, and he be to be put to death, *and thou hang him on a tree*: his body shall not remain all night upon the tree". It is at the cross of Christ that all the prodigal's deserts have been unsparingly meted out. There the obedient and devoted One stood in the sinner's place, and was made "sin" and "a curse" for us. He was forsaken of God, He drank the bitter cup of judgment to its dregs, and thus God has been glorified in righteousness, so that He is righteously free to take the prodigal into boundless favour.

God has raised Christ from the dead, and set Him at His own right hand. He there lives - glory-crowned - to the delight of God's heart, and on the ground of His work God is receiving prodigals into the favour and acceptance of which He alone is worthy. This is the key to Luke 15. You must have life, righteousness, and acceptance in Christ, or be for ever lost.

THE LAW, THE PROMISES, AND THE GOSPEL

Acts 13

It was after the reading of the law and the prophets that Paul stood up to preach the gospel. The law and the prophets were excellent in their place, but they did not meet the need of a sinner. The law brought home to men the knowledge of sin, and the prophets contained promises of grace and blessing to come. But neither the law nor the prophets really met the condition of men.

"By the law is the knowledge of sin". The law is the probe which shows the depth of the wound; it is the plumb-line which shows the crookedness of the wall; it is the candle which reveals all the filth and corruption of a sinner's heart; it is the sharp eye which detects the disease; it is the judge who passes sentence of "guilty before God" upon every member of the human family.

Then the prophets took it for granted that it was all over with man on the ground of law-keeping, and they were full of promises of future blessing on the ground of grace. The law had nothing but judgment for a sinner; the prophets had a promise of salvation for him. But a promise of deliverance is a very different thing from being delivered. The English residents in Lucknow during the Indian Mutiny, surrounded by thousands of foes who thirsted for their blood, had a promise of deliverance which, no doubt, filled their hearts with hope painful by its intensity, but it was a very different thing when they beheld their foes fleeing before the impetuous onslaught of the 78th Highlanders. Deliverance promised is a great thing, but deliverance accomplished is vastly greater. The prophets brought a promise of salvation, but the gospel declares that the promise has been fulfilled.

This is of great importance. For lack of seeing it many are strangers to the joy and peace of the gospel. “Of this man’s seed hath God according to promise raised unto Israel a Saviour, Jesus”. “And we declare unto you glad tidings, how that the promise which was made unto the fathers, God hath fulfilled the same unto us their children, in that he hath raised up Jesus” (verses 23, and 32, 33). The Spirit of God insists upon the fact that the promise has been fulfilled. Many a one will say, “I am trusting to the promises”. Well, it is good if their faith has laid hold of God’s grace in any measure, but there is a more excellent way. Indeed, those who talk thus will generally confess to having doubts and fears, more or less. They are really hoping for salvation instead of enjoying it. It cannot be otherwise. If someone promises you a book that you want you look forward with hope to the time when you will get it. You trust to the promise and hope for its fulfilment. But when the promise is fulfilled you cease to hope, and you enjoy that which was promised.

In the prophets we find many promises of salvation, such as, “I will also give thee for a light to the Gentiles, that thou mayest be my salvation unto the end of the earth” (Isaiah 49:6); and again, “All the ends of the earth shall see the salvation of our God” (Isaiah 52:10); and again, “It shall be said in that day, Lo, this is our God; we have waited for him, and he will save us: this is the Lord; we have waited for him, we will be glad and rejoice in his salvation” (Isaiah 25:9). So in Old Testament times it was “good that a man should both hope and quietly wait for the salvation of the Lord” (Lamentations 3). This was what Simeon and Anna were doing (Luke 2); but when the aged saint received the infant Jesus into his arms he said, “Now lettest thou thy servant depart in peace ... for mine eyes have seen thy salvation”. The promise was fulfilled: God had raised up a Saviour.

It is not now a question of promises but of a Person. “All the promises of God in Him are yea, and in Him, Amen”. Whatever promises of God there are, all are fulfilled in the Son of God. The value of a promissory note does not lie in the bit of paper, but in the person who has engaged himself thereby, and so salvation does not lie in the promises but in the Person who is the fulfilment of them all.

God has raised up a Saviour - Jesus - and is now sending out glad tidings concerning Him. "Whosoever among you feareth God, to you is the word of this salvation sent". If you have no fear of God before your eyes, you will care little for His salvation. But to those who have entered into fellowship with the dying thief - who addressed his railing comrade with the words, "Dost not thou fear God, seeing we are in the same condemnation? and we indeed justly" - the message of salvation is a joyful sound. Never was lifeboat more valued by the drowning, or fire-escape more welcomed by the inmates of a burning house than the message of salvation is valued and welcomed by the sinner who really fears God. If you want to know what it is to fear God read Psalm 51.

The rulers of Judæa had no thought that they were fulfilling the Scriptures when they condemned the Son of God. So far as they were concerned, they were gratifying the envy and hatred of their own wicked hearts, but God made the stormy wind of their evil passions to fulfil His word. They numbered Jesus with the transgressors, and appointed Him to death, though they found no cause of death in Him. Pilate said, "I am innocent of the blood of this just person"; the dying thief bore witness, "This man hath done nothing amiss"; the Spirit of God declared that He did no sin, neither was guile found in His mouth; and even Judas had to confess, "I have betrayed innocent blood". But in thus condemning the guiltless they were fulfilling the Scriptures. It was the will and purpose of God that Christ should suffer all that was written of Him, otherwise men would have had no power against Him at all. As it was, they fulfilled the prophets in condemning Him, and "having fulfilled all that was written of him, they laid him in a sepulchre".

"But God raised him from the dead". His atoning work was done: He had suffered for sins and died for sinners, and now God raised Him to be a Saviour in resurrection. He is now beyond the reach of Satan, beyond the touch of sin, beyond the power of death, in resurrection triumph, and this is the essence of the gospel.

The promises could refer to no other than Christ. The "sure mercies of David" were connected with One who was not to see corruption - One who was to be "as the light of the morning, when the sun riseth, even a morning without clouds" (2 Samuel 23:4, 5). And now the light of that cloudless resurrection morning has come. Death's dark night, which for a brief space enveloped the anointed One, has passed for ever, and He has risen as the Sun of an endless resurrection day. Death has won no spoil from Him; corruption - the emblem of death's victory - touched Him not. Blessed, victorious Saviour, well may sinners bow at Thy feet!

Now we get the proclamation of grace. "Be it known unto you, men and brethren, that through this man is preached unto you the forgiveness of sins". The grace that is thus presented to men can only be measured by the Person in whom it is set forth. If we think of His glory, His greatness, all His perfections, the infinite value of His atoning death, and His resurrection triumph, we may find sufficient cause and ground in Him for this blessed proclamation. Merit or excuse we have none. The accumulated burden of our sins might justly sink us to the lowest hell. But in Him we find One who is a propitiation for the whole world. On the ground of what He is, the forgiveness of sins can be universally proclaimed.

"And by him, all that believe are justified from all things from which ye could not be justified by the law of Moses". The law could not justify a sinner, but the grace of God justifies freely "through the redemption which is in Christ Jesus" (Romans 3:24). Will you not receive this forgiving and justifying grace? Will you not receive by faith the blessed Person in whom it is presented? He is placed before you in His attractiveness, and in His divine suitability to meet your need, that you may believe on Him and be saved. God puts no barrier between you and Christ;

"All the fitness He requireth,
Is to know your need of Him".

Let none persuade you that God is reluctant to bless, or that He needs to be moved to be gracious by long repentance and many prayers. Nay, verily, it is He who by His blessed gospel, and by the gracious strivings of His Spirit, is ever seeking to move men to repentance and faith in the Lord Jesus Christ. And when man's stubborn will yields to grace, and he confesses, "I have sinned", there is joy in the presence of the angels. God is a justifier and a Saviour God, and He delights to be known as such by His poor fallen creatures. If it were not so there would have been no risen Saviour - no proclamation of repentance and remission of sins among all nations beginning at Jerusalem (Luke 24:47).

"By him, all that believe are justified from all things". The divine clearance of the believer is perfect and unqualified. It leaves no unsettled questions behind, and therefore no element of unrest or uncertainty in the soul. "All things" covers the whole sinful history of the one who believes, with every particular detail of that history. Who can lay a charge against one of whom God declares that he is "justified from all things?" Of what avail are ten thousand accusing voices if God justifies? (Romans 8:33).

But bright lights cast dark shadows, and

if this pardoning and justifying grace be slighted it leaves the soul under greater condemnation. Take heed, then, to this solemn warning, “Beware, therefore, lest that come upon you which is spoken of in the prophets; Behold, ye despisers, and wonder, and perish: for I work a work in your days, a work which ye will in no wise believe, though a man declare it unto you”. God has wrought in the greatness of His grace, and has caused His gracious work to be declared unto you for the acceptance and obedience of faith. Be not a despiser of that grace, I beseech you, for it is still true that “whoso despiseth the word shall be destroyed”.

A THREEFOLD BLESSING

"*Giving thanks unto the Father, which hath made us meet to be partakers of the inheritance of the saints in light: who hath delivered us from the power of darkness, and hath translated us into the kingdom of his dear Son (the Son of love); in whom we have redemption through his blood, even the forgiveness of sine*". - Colossians 1:12 - 14.

These verses do not belong to everybody. They are the private property of the children of God - part of the title deeds of their inheritance. I open these precious records which declare the blessings of the children of God that there may arise in your heart a desire to be one of them. Thank God! His house and His heart are thrown open, and by His grace you may be one of His children, and may have the full assurance that the children's birthright is yours. How great is this grace! I trust you will not be indifferent to it.

The children of God are a people -

(1) Whose sins are forgiven, and who are redeemed from all the power of the enemy;

(2) Who are delivered from the world; and

(3) Who are made meet for glory.

What a wealth of blessing! And observe, it is all in connection with a Person. "*The Son of his love; in whom we have redemption through his blood, even the forgiveness of sins*". It is *through* and *in* a Person that we have all these things; and that Person is the Son of the Father's love, the Creator of all things, the mighty victor of Calvary, the Saviour of sinners. It is He who has stooped to secure, at an infinite cost, glory for God, and a boundless wealth of divine blessing for all who believe on His name. There is a Person who can meet all your need, and bring the brightness of divine love into your heart. If you knew that Person you could not help trusting Him. He loves to be trusted by the sinners for whom He died.

1. "Redemption through his blood, even the forgiveness of sins". *Sins*. Let us not hurry over that word. Let us give time for its echoes to be heard in our consciences. *Sins*. Unconverted friend, that word covers the whole of your history as seen by God, and when everything else is gone - friends, pleasures, business, all gone - sins will remain. You cannot deny you have sins; your conscience has its own solemn tale to tell about them. I daresay some sins blaze like beacon-fires in your memory; every backward glance brings them to view. It may be you have sins which you would give anything to blot out, but no regrets, or religious deeds, or penitential tears will remove the scarlet stains. There is but one door of hope - but

one avenue of escape available for you. Thank God! that way is wide open and free. Your sins, which are many, may be forgiven, and that in divine righteousness, *through His blood.* Satan's object is to defame the Saviour, and to belittle the value of His blood, by turning souls to their own works, or to sacraments, as a ground or means of pardon. But God has only one solution of the question of sin - only one ground on which He can forgive sins, and that is the death of Christ. It is "through his blood" *alone* that remission of sins may be had. When a sinner trusts in God he puts himself under shelter of the blood of Jesus; he takes his stand before God on the ground of that which has perfectly satisfied God; nay, more than that, he is on the ground of *God's own way of settling the tremendous questions of guilt and sin.* And the moment he takes that ground he has "the forgiveness of sins".

"In whom we have redemption". Redemption has to do with perfect deliverance from all the power of the enemy. The careless sinner is not troubled with doubts and fears; the object of the enemy is not to harass him, but to keep him in a delusive peace. It is *the anxious soul* who is beset by all kinds of difficulties. He wonders whether he has repented sufficiently, whether he has believed in the right way, whether God has really accepted him, or whether, after all, he is not deceiving himself. The soul in this state needs the knowledge of redemption, for redemption takes us completely out of the power of the one who holds us in this bondage. We have redemption *in a Person* - the Son of the Father's love. It is on the ground of the shedding of His blood that we have it, but it is *in Him.* Our sins are removed by His blood, but our standing with God is measured by the Person whose blood has cleansed us.

Where is our Saviour? He was once upon the cross; He felt there the unspeakable anguish of being forsaken by God; and He bowed His head in death. As to the expiation of sins, all was accomplished in that dark and solemn hour when He was lifted up. But He is risen and is now in glory. The diadems of victory are on His blessed brow as He sits at the right hand of God, and He is there for us. It is *in that glory-crowned Person* that we have redemption. Our Saviour lives, and we have redemption in Him.

The power of the enemy over you depends upon his ability to occupy you with yourself; and indeed your heart is so foolish that it may be turned aside by the smallest bit of sin or folly, and this gives the enemy occasion to assault you, and to question the reality of the work of God in your soul. But when you have looked at yourself long enough to discover that you are only fit for the lake of fire, you are glad to turn from yourself to your risen Saviour. While the everlasting ages roll there can be no change in Him, and our place and standing with God are measured by Him. You rest upon His blood, but you look up to where He is in heavenly glory, and you say, "Thank God! I have redemption *in Him*".

2. "Who hath delivered us from the power of darkness, and hath translated us into the kingdom of the Son of his love". The world is "the power of darkness". It is a system of things which wraps itself with awful power round the hearts and consciences of sinners, and holds them in a terrible bondage as they speed on to the lake of fire. Alas! there are many who profess to be Christians who have never accepted God's deliverance from the world. Fancy a novel-reader or a theatre-goer calling himself a Christian! Yet there are such people to be found. It is an awful thing for a Christian to be found enjoying the things which are only designed to lead souls to destruction. The world is the gilded and flower-bedecked cage in which Satan carries his victims to the lake of fire. It is dreadful to think of a worldly Christian! Let each one ask himself, "Am I going on with the things which led to the death of my Saviour?" How can we look for happiness in the pleasures of the world? The rejectors and murderers of Christ are trying to be happy without Him; indeed, in His presence they would be most miserable. Shall we join them in their ungodly mirth? Surely not. We look for our happiness in another scene, where our Saviour sits at the right hand of God.

God has revealed the Son of His love to our hearts, and the knowledge of that blessed Person carries our affections out of the world. The idols that once charmed us are forgotten, or only remembered with shame. We are translated "into the kingdom of the Son of his love". There are only two companies on earth - one under the control of Satan, and the other under the control of the Son of the Father's love. One of the greatest blessings of the gospel is that God puts the believer under the authority of the One who has saved him. We have now to please but One. In His known love He bears sway over our hearts.

3. "Giving thanks unto the Father, which hath made us meet to be partakers of the inheritance of the saints in light".

The Father has made us meet for glory. Nothing would suit His heart but this. We shall ever be in the Father's presence clothed in the beauty of Christ, and He has brought it all about for His own pleasure, and for the satisfaction of His own love. Christ has been made sin for us that we might become the righteousness of God in Him. The Father would have the feeblest believer in Jesus to know the love that thus invests him with meetness for heavenly light. Stand still, thou returning prodigal, and see how love arrays thee! As the hymn says -

"Put them on me - robes of glory,
Spotless as the heavens above;
Not to meet my thoughts of fitness,
But His wondrous thoughts of love".

It is in the Father's heart to have "many sons" around Himself in heavenly glory in the unsullied light of His own holiness and love. For this He "hath made us meet". We shall be in the Father's house for ever, in company with the Son whose work has fitted us to be there in perfect suitability to the place. And while here on earth, we have the Spirit of sonship, crying, "Abba, Father". Well may we say, in the words of olden time, "Happy is that people that is in such a case".

A TRIUMPHANT SAVIOUR

Luke 8:26-56

The whole gospel of Luke may be epitomised in one verse of Scripture: "God anointed Jesus of Nazareth with the Holy Ghost and with power: who went about doing good, and healing all that were oppressed of the devil; for God was with him" (Acts 10:38). The Son of God is seen here in lowly grace, and in the mighty power of God, triumphing over all the power of sin and Satan, and removing the effects of that power by which man was oppressed. It is really God coming in on behalf of man against all the power of evil under which man has fallen. In short, it is the revelation of God as a Saviour God.

Man as a fallen creature is strong to do evil, powerless to do good, and in consequence subject to death. He is the slave of the *power* of sin, he suffers from the *plague* of sin, and he is subject to the *penalty* of sin. The Lord Jesus is here presented to us, in figure, as One who can break the power of sin, heal the plague of sin, and abolish the penalty of sin.

I take this poor demoniac in Luke 8 as a figure of man controlled by the active energy of evil. He was the slave and victim of an evil power which he had no will to resist, and from whose tyranny he could not escape. He might fancy himself strong and free to take his own course, but he was really altogether yielded to the evil power that controlled him.

How solemn is that word of the Lord, "Verily, verily, I say unto you, Whosoever committeth sin is the servant [slave] of sin!" (John 8:34). Surely this comes home to every conscience. Then again the Spirit of God says, "Know ye not, that to whom ye yield yourselves servants [slaves] to obey, his servants [slaves] ye are to whom ye obey; whether of sin unto death, or of obedience unto righteousness?" (Romans 6:16). Sin is a terrible power to which man yields his affections and energies, and by which he is carried along in disobedience and independence of God. Men think that they are only giving effect to their own desires as they live in self-will, but in reality they are yielding themselves to a power of evil which is bent on their destruction.

Looking at the demoniac as a figure of man yielded to the power of sin, I want to call attention to three facts about him.

1. *He "ware no clothes"*. Clothing in Scripture is symbolical of righteousness. For example, it is written, "He hath clothed me with the garments of salvation, he hath covered me with the robe of righteousness" (Isaiah 61:10). It is because man has fallen under the power of sin that righteousness is necessary for

him. Man in innocence needed no clothing. But the moment Adam had sinned, he became conscious that he needed something to fit him for God's presence. When once sin had come in there could be no return to innocence, and man's need could only be met by "the gift of righteousness" (Romans 5:17). No self-made aprons of fig-leaves will suffice; man's most earnest efforts to put himself right are unavailing, and in spite of them all he remains "naked" before God.

But "unto Adam also and to his wife did the Lord God make coats of skins, and clothed them" (Genesis 3:21). On this early page of man's history we see, in striking picture, righteousness provided by God for man, and this upon the ground of the death of another. Man can only have righteousness on the ground that sin's full penalty has been paid. Christ has died for sinners, so that as risen from the dead He might become the righteousness of all who believe. Those who believe on God, who raised up Jesus our Lord from the dead, receive "the gift of righteousness". Christ is the believer's righteousness (see 1 Corinthians 1:30; Romans 10:4). Have you received this priceless gift? Or are you still, as a guilty and wilful sinner, "found naked" before God?

2. *He dwelt "in the tombs"*. Man as yielded to the power of sin was driven out of Paradise (Genesis 3:24) into a world characterized by defilement and death, and Adam's children

dwell there unto this day. Death has "passed upon all men, for that all have sinned"; its blight rests on every pleasure, on every accession of wealth or honour, on all that is dear to man's heart. Soon - very soon - all must be left. Death follows hard upon the footsteps of those who walk in the counsel of the ungodly. Mercy may hold him back for a season, but soon death's rough hand will be laid upon the sinner - the one who is a servant "of sin unto death".

3. *He wanted nothing to do with Jesus.* This is the crowning proof that man is the willing servant of the power of evil. Not only does he rebel against God's authority and transgress God's commandments, but when God comes near to him in grace as a Saviour God he despises and rejects Him. If I were asked to give an example of the power of sin I would not point to the thief, the drunkard, or the profligate. These are examples patent to every eye. I would rather describe an upright, amiable, and altogether well-behaved person, who prefers the world and its things to the Lord Jesus Christ and the all-blessing grace of God. Little things, and what people call innocent things, may keep the soul from Christ. But can anything be called innocent that keeps a precious and immortal soul from the knowledge of God in grace? No! depend upon it, that which does so is nothing but the awful power of sin, however it may disguise itself. Little things that hold the heart in the world are often more deadly

than greater evils, for the conscience slumbers over them while grave iniquities would awaken it to activity.

But is there not deliverance for man from this terrible power of evil under which he has fallen? Yes, thank God, there is, and we see it pictured in the scene before us. Deliverance came to the poor demoniac in the Person and power of the Lord Jesus. There was One who could bid the demons depart and restore their unhappy victim to "his right mind". How blessed to see this! There is a gracious power by which man may be set free from the power of evil; and that gracious power is set forth by the gospel unto all men. It is made available for men. The gospel is "the power of God unto salvation to every one that believeth" (Romans 1:16).

God's deliverance for man is set forth in His Son Jesus Christ our Lord. God has taken into consideration the whole state of men as under the power of sin, and has provided everything in grace for their relief and blessing. And those who receive this grace obtain freedom from the power of sin.

In the first place God furnishes righteousness for man through the Lord Jesus Christ. He makes no claim upon us, but sets One before us who suffered for sins upon the cross, and who, as made sin for us, has glorified God, so that repentance and remission of sins might be proclaimed to us in His name. He provides righteousness for us in a risen Saviour, and declares that "by him all that believe are justified from all things, from which ye could not be justified by the law of Moses" (Acts 13:39).

Then, further, in revealing Himself as a Saviour, God has shown that it is His pleasure to have men in His favour. If the earthly Eden is for ever lost, another and a fairer scene is thrown open. For the favour into which men are brought by the grace of God is nothing less than that which rests upon the risen Christ. If we are justified by faith, and have peace with God through our Lord Jesus Christ, we are also entitled through Him to "have access into this grace [favour] wherein we stand, and rejoice in hope of the glory of God" (Romans 5:1, 2). What a contrast to "the tombs"! The psalmist could say, "In his favour is life: weeping may endure for a night, but joy cometh in the morning" (Psalm 30:5). The believer's life is in the favour of God, and the object of his hope is the glory of God.

God, thus known in infinite grace, becomes the joy and boast of those who believe. We "joy in God through our Lord Jesus Christ". As a Saviour God He has provided for our need. He has relieved us of all that pressed upon us. He has justified us, set us in His favour according to the acceptance of Christ, and enriched us with abundance of grace. It is in this wondrous and blessed grace that God is revealed in the gospel. Does it attract your heart? Are you glad to think that God is such a One? Will you not turn now to the God who has thus in grace provided every blessing for man? All, all may be yours. This infinite grace is for all who will receive it as a divine gift through faith in the Lord Jesus Christ.

The delivered man, sitting at the feet of Jesus, clothed, and in his right mind, presents a lovely picture of the effect produced when a man comes "under grace". The power of evil no longer controls him; he has found relief and peace and blessing in the knowledge of God; and he now yields himself to God as one who is alive from the dead, and his members as instruments of righteousness to God (Romans 6:13, 14).

Sin is a *power* terrible as that of a legion of demons, but it is also a *plague* in the soul which renders men incapable of doing the will of God, even when, through grace, they have a desire to do what is good. The woman with the issue of blood represents the weakness of the flesh. She had a strong desire to be well, and to escape from the disabilities of her condition, but she had to prove that all human aid was in vain. Thus she represented one who is born anew, and has the will to do good, but not the power (Romans 7:18-24).

The secret history of many a soul is portrayed

in that of this woman. Their conduct may be exemplary to a high degree, their practical life almost blameless, and yet they have the abiding consciousness of weakness and failure. They have an acute sense of the claims of divine holiness, and a crushing weight of self-condemnation rests on their spirits as they realise their own terrible imperfection. They are ready to turn to anything that seems to promise more power, but every expedient fails them. They have to learn that there is nothing but death in themselves (Romans 7:24), and that they must find the power of life in Another.

She "came behind him, and touched the border of his garment: and immediately her issue of blood stanched". The moment she came into connection with Him there was an end of the infirmity. "Virtue" went out of Him for her healing. We have to realise that in us, that is, in our flesh, good does not dwell, but we find grace and power in Another - in Christ Jesus. On our side we need everything: on His side there is the supply of everything. All divine resources of grace and strength for the support and succour of saints reside in Him. How good it is to touch the border of His garment - to come into connection with all the gracious power that resides in Him! The moment we look altogether away from ourselves for deliverance and the power of life we find it in Him. When we really come to the consciousness that we need a deliverer outside ourselves, we find One in Him (see Romans 7:24, 25).

And "virtue" comes out of Him by the Spirit for our support. All His grace and sufficiency are made good to us by the Spirit. In this way we are made capable for the will of God, so that "the righteousness of the law might be fulfilled in us, who walk not after the flesh, but after the Spirit" (Romans 8:4). Thus by divine grace and power we are made superior to the weakness of the flesh. The plague, in that sense, is healed. Not that flesh is made spiritual; it remains flesh; but by the power of Christ through the Spirit we are sustained in superiority to its weakness.

The third feature of man's condition as a fallen creature is that he is subject to death, the penalty of sin. Of this we have a figure in the daughter of Jairus, and in connection with her being raised up we see a picture of the Lord Jesus as the One who "hath abolished death, and hath brought life and immortality to light through the gospel" (2 Timothy 1:10). Any measure of grace or mercy which stopped short of removing the penalty of sin would be of small value to man. Yet there are many people who think highly of providential mercies, but hardly bestow a thought on the grace that has come in to relieve men of the penalty of sin.

The way which grace took to effect this great deliverance is suggested by the words, "he took her by the hand". The blessed Son of God came into personal contact with death. One who was personally exempt from death became subject to it by the grace of God. There was no mitigation of the penalty when the sinless One was made sin for us. But the greatness and glory of His Person were the sure pledge of complete victory. It was not possible that He could be holden of death. The fact that He went into it ensured complete deliverance for all who believe on Him. He has annulled death, and now life and incorruptibility are brought to light in Him, the risen and glorified Saviour. The penalty of sin has been removed in the death of Christ for all who believe on His name, and "the gift of God is eternal life in Christ Jesus our Lord" (Romans 6:23).

May God bring you to know this triumphant Saviour, in whom there is such a perfect and divine answer to all your need as a sinner.

THE BEGINNING OF A BLISSFUL ETERNITY

It is not possible for a believer to be entirely free from doubts and misgivings until he sees that his righteousness and his place with God are set forth in Christ. When he does see this it settles every question, and puts the soul altogether beyond the reach of the enemy.

Let me put this matter in a very simple way. Suppose you were to die and to pass the judgment-throne, and that you found yourself on the other side of death and judgment without a stain of sin upon you, and not only "whiter than snow", but in all the acceptance and beauty of Christ, and with the smile of God's eternal favour beaming upon you, would you not be sure that every question was settled? Would you not be able to say, "Thank God, this is the beginning of a blissful eternity"? Would you not be assured of the love and favour of God?

Well, now, let me turn your eye to *another Person*. You are not actually beyond death and judgment, but Christ is. In deep, divine love He entered into death and bore the judgment of God. He "was delivered for our offences, and raised again for our justification". All that was due to us passed upon Him; He has endured and exhausted it all, so that the believer can sing -

"Death and judgment are behind me".

And now Christ is our righteousness; we are received by God in all His acceptance. Thus we enter into everlasting favour. We think not of ourselves, but of Christ. I am not beyond death and judgment, but *Christ* is, and I am entitled to know by faith that He was raised for my justification. What a blessed answer to every doubt and fear is found in that risen Christ!

If you read Romans 4 and 5 you will see how wondrously God has wrought that we might know Him and trust Him as the God of our salvation. We believe on God "that raised up Jesus our Lord from the dead". It was God who gave Him to die; and when all the blessed work of atonement was finished God raised Him from the dead for our justification, so that "being justified by faith" we might "have peace with God through our Lord Jesus Christ". God has settled every question in His own way and at His own cost. We believe on God; it is not only that we believe texts of Scripture, but we believe on God.

We believe *on God* (Romans 4:24)
We have peace *with God* (Romans 5:1).
We are reconciled *to God* (Romans 5:10)
We joy *in God* (Romans 5:11)

These four things give us in a very full and blessed way the portion of the believer. God is the object of his faith and the source of his joy. He has begun with God, and that is the beginning of a blissful eternity.

THE WATER OF LIFE

"I will give unto him that is athirst of the fountain of the water of life freely". - Revelation 21:6

"Whosoever will, let him take the water of life freely". - Revelation 22:17

Nothing could be more solemn and striking, or more exquisite in grace, than the way the "water of life" is presented in these closing chapters of the Holy Scriptures.

Two scenes are set before us - one of unmingled bliss, where God is all in all, and another of unutterable woe, far away from His presence. In Revelation 21:1-8 time has ceased to be; the long centuries of this world's sad and tragic history have closed; God's eternity has come, with all its happiness for the redeemed. For "the tabernacle of God is with men, and he will dwell with them, and they shall be his people, and God himself shall be with them, and be their God. And God shall wipe away all tears from their eyes; and there shall be no more death, neither sorrow, nor crying, neither shall there be any more pain: for the former things are passed away". Blessed eternity, where all things are of God, and God is all in all, and everything responds to God!

Then there is another scene. "But the fearful,

and unbelieving, and the abominable, and murderers, and whore-mongers, and sorcerers, and idolaters, and all liars, shall have their part in the lake which burneth with fire and brimstone which is the second death". Woeful eternity of the lost! Far from peace, and light, and love; far, far from God. Solemn, awful eternity!

Between these two scenes we find the precious words, "I will give unto him that is athirst of the fountain of the water of life freely". How suggestive is this. You can only reach the scene where God is all in all by drinking of the fountain of the water of life. Only by drinking of that fountain can you escape having your part in the scene which is far from God.

The heart of an unconverted man or woman, or boy or girl, is very like that awful scene in a lost eternity. That is, God has no place in it. "There is no fear of God before their eyes". "The fool hath said in his heart, No God". If we could explore the heart of an unconverted person we should find business, pleasures, friends, hobbies, lusts, and folly, but no God. As the Scripture saith, "God is not in all his thoughts". And remember everyone goes "to his own place". If God has no place in your heart, your place must be in the scene that is far from God. God will get a place in your heart if you drink of the fountain of the water of life. Thank God, you are still within reach of that blessed fountain.

Surely you know what it is to be "athirst". You try to make yourself happy, and to think that you are happy, but there is a void in your heart. Business, pleasures, and, it may be, religion have failed to quench the thirst of your soul; and an eternity lies before you which may be one of *quenchless thirst.* But at this moment God is saying in the tenderness of infinite love, "I will give unto him that is athirst of the fountain of the water of life freely". What you need is the knowledge of God. Divine love alone can quench the thirst of your soul. I knew a gentleman who went three times round the world in search of satisfaction, but never found it until he drank of "the fountain of the water of life".

We have many examples in Scripture of those who thirsted and who drank of the fountain. Nicodemus was one. He "came to Jesus by night, and said unto him, Rabbi, we know that thou art a teacher come from God: for no man can do these miracles that thou doest, except God be with him" (John 3:2). He was thirsting for the knowledge of God.

Many were coming in the daytime with a merely external interest in the miracles; but Nicodemus came by night, that he might be alone with Jesus, and that he might hear of God. He was a rich man, a great religious dignitary, and no doubt well versed in Scripture, but he came as a little child to sit at the feet of Jesus. The "master of Israel" humbled himself to be taught by One who was of no account in the estimation of men in general. All his greatness and pride had completely broken down, and he was athirst for God. He came to drink of the fountain of the water of life.

In the millennium a "pure *river* of water of life" will flow out in blessing from the throne of God and of the Lamb. But today it is not a river, but a *fountain*. A fountain is the source of a river. You might drink of a river thousands of miles from its source; and so in the millennium there will be many who will taste of the blessing that flows out from God, but they will be a long way from the source, they will not really know God at all. But if you get any blessing today, you must get it from the very *Source* - you must drink of "the *fountain* of the water of life". The heart of God is the *source* of blessing.

Nicodemus thirsted, and God gave to him of the fountain of the water of life. The Son of God told him of a love which *would reach man and bless man through death*. "As Moses lifted up the serpent in the wilderness, even so must the Son of man be lifted up: that whosoever believeth in him should not perish, but have eternal life. For God loved the world, that he gave his only begotten Son, that whosoever believeth in him should not perish, but have everlasting life". Here we are brought to the fountain of the water of life, to the eternal springs of love in the heart of God. The Son of God told the story of a love which could only reach man through death - of a love which would bring its subjects into eternal life. He told it in *word* to Nicodemus, and He told it in *deed* on the cross. There was an absolute necessity for death if the love of God was to reach us, for our lives were forfeited - death was upon us - the Son of man *must* be lifted up. God's love has told itself out in death - death is the witness of that love; He sent His Son to die. And if you are "athirst" this blessed revelation of God is for you. You may drink into this love until all your soul is satisfied. As you drink of the fountain of the water of life your heart receives the knowledge of God. God in His known and trusted love gets a place in your heart, and it becomes your joy to anticipate an eternity in which He will be all in all.

The woman of Samaria was another thirsting soul, but of a very different type. Nicodemus had been seeking to quench his thirst in a religious way, but she, like many others, had been trying to do it by self-gratification. The blessed Lord had to bring her to the consciousness of what it was she really needed. Nothing but the knowledge of God could satisfy her thirsting heart. Jesus speaks to her of the giving God, and of the living water which should be in the one who drank of it as "a well of water springing up into everlasting life". Then He reaches her conscience, and makes her realise that it is with God she has to do. And, finally, He makes Himself known to her as the One who tells "all things", not only the "all things that ever I did", but the "all things" comprised in the perfect revelation of God (compare verse 29 with verse 25). She found herself at the fountain of the water of life, and she drank and was satisfied. How delighted would God be to make good to you such a blessed revelation of Himself, that your fears would be all dismissed, and your thoughts of self-gratification would lose their power as that revelation became by the Holy Spirit the life of your soul.

The last note of the silver trumpet of grace is now sounding out: "Whosoever will, let him take the water of life freely". It is free *for all* - free for you. It is God's deep joy to find an empty, thirsting soul who is willing to "take the water of life". The love that has told itself out in the death of Christ becomes the satisfaction of every heart that really knows it. In heaven that love will pervade everything with its ineffable sweetness and power. All things will be made new, that there may be nothing unsuited to divine love. And God will be "all in all". Everyone there will have taken the water of life, everyone will know God in the blessedness of His nature, every heart will be eternally filled and satisfied with the love which has told itself out in the gift and death of the Son of God.

But the joy of heaven may be known now - the atmosphere of the Father's house may be breathed even here, for "God is love; and he that dwelleth in love dwelleth in God, and God in him" (1 John 4:16). Then drink, anxious soul, at the fountain so free; and let those who have believed through grace drink deeper still. "The Lord direct your hearts into the love of God".

CONVICTED AND SIFTED

Luke 5:1-11; Luke 22:31-34

There are few characters in Scripture more interesting, or more profitable to study, than that of Simon Peter. I wish to bring before you at this time two scenes in his life which vividly illustrate God's ways in grace with sinners and with failing saints.

We have no means of knowing what kind of man Simon was before he became a disciple of Christ, though we may gather that he was a conscientious and God-fearing Jew from the fact that he could say, "I have never eaten anything that is common or unclean" (Acts 10:14). Nothing leads us to suppose that he was an immoral or irreligious man. He was, nevertheless, *a sinner*, and Luke 5:1-11 tells us how he came to be convicted of sin.

The Lord Jesus was teaching by the side of the lake, and such numbers gathered to hear the word of God, that they pressed upon Him. Whereupon He stepped into Simon's boat and - asking him to thrust out a little from the shore - sat down and taught the multitude out of the boat. It does not appear that the sermon took much effect upon Simon, but what happened afterwards wrought a complete revolution in his soul.

When Jesus had left speaking to the people, He turned to Simon, and said, "Launch out into the deep, and let down your nets for a draught". Simon did not seem to have much faith, for he said, "Master, we have toiled all the night, and have taken nothing: nevertheless, at thy word I will let down the net". No sooner had they done so than the net was filled, even to breaking, with fish; and when they began to gather them in, so great was the quantity that the boats began to sink. To the bystanders it was a miracle to wonder at; to the fishermen it was also a matter to rejoice over; but to Simon's conscience it brought the light of God's presence. He became conscious in the depths of his soul that he was in the presence of God, and along with that came the deep conviction of his utter unfitness to be there.

Such an experience has been, or will be, the experience of every human soul. The moment a sinner is brought consciously into the presence of God, he knows he is not fit to be there. Simon cried, "Depart from me, for I am a sinful man, O Lord". So long as a man walks in his own little circle, and in the light of sparks of his own kindling, he may talk with great swelling words, and have much self-confidence. But let him be brought consciously into God's presence, and in the soul-searching light of that presence the only thought left in his heart will be, "I am utterly unfit to be here".

The light of God makes things manifest as they

really are. The sinner out of God's presence may be well-pleased with himself; but the moment he comes into the light, every bit of self-righteousness and self-satisfaction withers up as the moth's flimsy wing shrivels in the flame. His comeliness is turned into corruption, and all his self-complacent thoughts and feelings give place to the supreme conviction, "I am a sinful man".

We see a remarkable illustration of this in the life of Job. In moral excellence Job stood head and shoulders above all his fellow-men. His good works were innumerable; his patience has passed into a proverb for all succeeding ages; but he had never truly seen himself in the light of God. Hence we find whole chapters filled with speeches in which he gives an account of his own goodness, and in chapter 27: 6, he declares, "My righteousness I hold fast, and will not let it go". But how soon did he change his opinion when the Lord came down and spoke to him out of the whirlwind! When the Lord had finished speaking, "Job answered the Lord, and said, Behold I am vile" (Job 40:3, 4).

He had seen the Lord, and had seen himself in the light of the Lord's presence, and instead of talking about his goodness any longer, he says, "Now mine eye seeth thee. Wherefore I abhor myself, and repent in dust and ashes" (Job 42:5, 6).

Those who have never thus had to do with God cannot understand the self-loathing, and the oppression of conscience which convicted sinners feel. A man in distress about his soul went to a clergyman for advice. The clergyman - himself an unconverted man - was greatly alarmed to witness his anguish of soul, and asked if he had murdered somebody! Job had not been doing anything outrageous. He had neither been stealing, swearing, telling lies, getting drunk, nor anything that men would call evil, but in the presence of God he found himself to be vile. The same effect is produced whenever a sinner is brought consciously into the light of God. He has no longer any excuses to make, or any merit to plead. His mouth is stopped, and he stands guilty before God.

To a convicted and repentant sinner the grace of God is exceedingly attractive. Wherever there is divine conviction there is also divine attraction. This accounts for the apparent inconsistency of Simon, who "fell down at Jesus' knees, saying, Depart from me". He knew that he was sinful and unfit for God, but the grace of God attracted him and secured his blessing.

"And Jesus Said unto Simon, Fear not: from henceforth thou shalt catch men". As soon as Simon took his place as a sinful man in the presence of the Lord, he got a word to dismiss his fears. In the Lord Jesus Christ there is not only light to reveal what man is but grace that delights to meet all man's need. When a sinner comes to himself in the presence of God, he learns that his wretchedness and need brought the Son of God from heaven to die. This is what the self-righteous man can never understand. It is a mystery of grace that convicted sinners learn at the feet of Jesus.

When Jesus went into the house of Zacchæus, the people "murmured, saying, That he was gone to be guest with a man that is a sinner". He replied, "The Son of man is come to seek and to save that which was lost". The Great Physician came not to go through the mockery of pretending to heal those who were well, or but slightly indisposed. He came to undertake and accomplish the cure of those whose case was desperate, and beyond all other aid. Simon took his place as "a sinful man", and immediately the Saviour of the sinful said, "Fear not". Oh! the sweetness of the gospel of the grace of God! The light of God discloses my sin; the grace of God provides an all-sufficient Saviour for me in the Person of His Son. I can only stand astonished in presence of the holiness that brings all my sins to light, and the infinite grace that puts them for ever out of sight.

That this grace of God might "reign through righteousness" it was necessary that the Lord Jesus should die. "It behoved Christ to suffer, and to rise from the dead the third day: and that repentance and remission of sins should be preached in his name among all nations, beginning at Jerusalem" (Luke 24:46, 47). And now that He is risen and glorified, the divine proclamation runs, "Be it known unto you therefore, men and brethren, that through this man is preached unto you the forgiveness of sins: and by him all that believe are justified from all things, from which ye could not be justified by the law of Moses" (Acts 13:38, 39).

"But", says one, "I am such a sinner!" Then you, at any rate, are called, for Jesus says, "I am not come to call the righteous, *but sinners* to repentance". And again He says, "Him that cometh to me I will *in no wise* cast out". Oh that you would come to Him just as you are, and receive the forgiveness of sins which is proclaimed in His name!

Mark the effect of the grace of God upon Simon. "When they had brought their ships to land, they forsook all and followed him". The grace of God had come to them in a Person, and that Person henceforth became everything to their hearts. The One who said, "Fear not", also said, "Follow me"; and in glad response "they forsook all and followed him". Other things were not worthy of a thought in comparison with Him. This is the legitimate effect of knowing the Lord Jesus as Saviour. When He says, "Fear not", the burden is gone, and the One who removed it acquires a place of supremacy in the affections. When conviction of sin has been deep and real, and the Lord Jesus is known as the One who has silenced all accusations and removed all fears, He becomes everything to the soul that thus knows Him.

I have heard of a slave who was being carried by sea to some market to be sold. An English merchant on the same vessel noticed and pitied him, and finally determined, if possible, to set him free. On inquiring the price, he found it would take all the profits of his voyage to redeem the slave, but he paid down the money, and the poor creature became his property. The slave's eyes burned with anger when he heard what had taken place. Said he to the merchant, "Are you an Englishman, and a lover of liberty? Have you not even pretended to pity my miserable condition? And now you buy me for your slave!" "Yes", said the merchant, with tears in his eyes, "I have bought you, but now I set you free; you are at liberty to do as you like". The ransomed slave fell at his feet, and cried, "Master, I will follow and serve you as long as I live".

This illustrates the effect of redemption being fully known. Every saved one will bear me out in this, that when the grace of God and redemption in Christ Jesus was first realised by them, that blessed One had a place in their hearts before and above everything else. We heard His "Fear not"; we rejoiced in His call, "Follow me"; and we felt that we wanted Him to take captive every affection of our hearts, and reign without a rival there. This is the divine effect of grace being known in the believer's heart.

Another scene in Simon's history now claims our attention (Luke 22:31-34). The deep and humiliating experience of weakness and failure through which he passed in the high priest's house was a sifting never to be forgotten. The details are, no doubt, well known to us all. I do not dwell upon them. You remember the self-confident spirit that boasted, and the presumptuous daring that slighted warning, and ventured to its fall. You have seen weakness that quailed in the moment of trial before a scoffing maid, and you can understand the anguish of the poor disciple's heart as he "went out and wept bitterly". A human biographer would have drawn a veil over such a scene and let it be forgotten. Not so the Spirit of God. One of the few things that God has seen fit to record in all the four gospels, is the story of Peter's denial of the Lord. Why is this? Is it because God loves to recall the failure of His saints? Nay, verily; but because Peter's fall was used by divine grace to bring about a great and needed change in his estimate of himself, without which he could never have been a pillar in the church or a strengthener of his brethren.

There was with Simon, as with us all, a degree of self-confidence which needed to be broken down. In his case it was the self-confidence of an ardent and devoted nature, and of one whose true affection for the Lord carried him into danger and temptation. But "the flesh profiteth nothing", and Simon had to learn this as sifted by Satan.

There are two ways in which we may discover the worthlessness of the flesh - we may be winnowed by Christ, or sifted by Satan. John the baptist spoke of the coming Messiah as One whose fan was in His hand, and who would thoroughly purge His floor. I do not now go into the meaning of this as applied to Israel, but simply call your attention to the fact that Christ *winnows*, whereas Satan sifts. The effect of winnowing is that the chaff is driven away, and the wheat remains. In the presence of the Lord, and in subjection of spirit to Him, we may learn what the flesh is in communion with Him. This will make us very distrustful of ourselves, and lead us to walk in self-judgment, and in result the flesh will be practically displaced. But if our wills are allowed to work, and the natural self-confidence of our hearts does not find itself rebuked in the presence of the Lord, we must needs (like Simon) be sifted by Satan, and learn by painful experience the lesson we have failed to learn in communion. When Satan sifts, it is not to get rid of the chaff but of the wheat. He would like every grain of wheat to fall through, so that the sieve might be full of chaff. He would like to make it appear as if there was nothing of God in the saint.

Satan leads the self-confident saint into temptation, overthrows him, and then says, “There now, a fine Christian you are, to have done a thing like that! After the profession you have made, too, and the way you have talked! Did you not even say you never could do a thing like that? And now you have done it! It is clear you have been nothing but a hypocrite all the time you were pretending to be a saint!”

Then he will shift his ground a little and say, “Now you see it is no use trying to be a Christian. You have tried, and this is the end of it. Instead of being happy you are more miserable now than before you were converted. You had better give it all up, and enjoy the world while you have the chance”. So Satan uses the saint’s failure to lead him, if possible, to *despair of Christ*. But God uses it to teach him *distrust of self.* And it is exceedingly precious to see how the Lord deals in divine grace with the failing one.

“I have prayed for thee, *that thy faith fail not*”. God will have self-confidence broken down, but He carefully sustains the souls of His saints, so that, while a fall breaks self-confidence, it is not suffered to destroy confidence in Him. The intercession of Christ secures this, that however great the failure of a true saint may be, his confidence in God never wholly fails.

"The Lord turned and looked upon Peter". If the question were to be put round amongst believers, "How is a failing saint restored?" not a few would reply, "By repentance and confession". Quite true! so far as our side of it goes, but there must be something *to produce* repentance and confession, and nothing will do that but the active love of the Lord Jesus Himself. Restoration begins with Him - "He looked upon Peter". Oh, what a Saviour is ours! The very failure and sin which is our shame brings us to prove His unfailing love, for it is written, "If any man sin, we have an advocate with the Father, Jesus Christ the righteous" (1 John 2:1). Before confession, before repentance, there is the activity of His grace.

Is my reader a backslidden and worldly believer? The eyes of your Saviour and Lord are upon you now. In all the tenderness of that love which carried Him to the cross, He is looking upon you from the glory. Yes! your denied and dishonoured Lord loves you still. May the warmth of His matchless love thaw your ice-bound heart! "And Peter went out, and wept bitterly". Backslider, remember from whence thou art fallen, and repent!

The Spirit of God has drawn a veil over the experiences of Peter during the three days that elapsed between the denial and the resurrection. His faith, sustained in answer to the prayer of the blessed Intercessor, did not fail. He remained with the brethren, but the anguish of his spirit must have been great. The Lord is faithful and He loves His own too well to spare the discipline and correction that they need. But our hearts may well adore the wisdom and the grace in which He watches, as the refiner of silver, the furnace in which they are tested and purified. He will have all the dross purged away, but He watches with the solicitude of divine love lest the precious metal should receive injury in the process.

When the poor fornicator at Corinth had been brought to self-judgment and repentance, the saints were besought to forgive him, and comfort him, and to confirm their love toward him, lest he should be swallowed up with overmuch sorrow. It appears to me that the same gracious love dictated the message of Mark 16:7, "Tell his disciples *and Peter*". What an assurance of unabated affection! A special message, by name, from the risen Lord to Peter! Surely that message, while it reassured the penitent heart, must have broken it afresh by its tenderness of love!

"The Lord is risen indeed, and hath appeared to Simon" (Luke 24:34). This scripture makes it plain that before Jesus met with His disciples, or had been seen by the ten, He granted a private interview to Simon. The believer's confession of sin is not for the ears of the world, nor does the Lord throw open everything to the gaze even of his brethren. Many things have to be exposed in public, simply because we have not had to say to the Lord in private about them. A heart beating, as Peter's did, with true affection for the Lord, could not rest without having all out with Him. And in many cases these disclosures and confessions would remain a personal secret between the Lord and our hearts.

But confession is not restoration, though it is essential to restoration. We are not restored by confession, but by the Lord, and in John 21:15-22 we see the manner of His gracious acting for Simon's entire restoration.

In the first place Simon was probed to the depths of his heart to discover whether his self-confidence was effectually destroyed. Three times had he denied his Lord, and three times a searching question, in different forms, was applied to him. "Simon, son of Jonas, lovest thou me more than these? You once professed greater love than all, Simon; is it so?". Ah! he was now "converted"; he dare no longer boast; he can only say, "Yea, Lord, *thou knowest* that I have affection for thee". "Simon, son of Jonas, lovest thou me?" No longer, Do you love Me more than these? but, Do you love Me at all? Peter replies, "Yea, Lord *thou knowest* that I have affection for thee". "Simon, son of Jonas, hast thou affection for me? After what has happened, can you say you have affection for Me?" Peter was grieved ("sorrowful") and said unto Him, "Lord, *thou knowest all things*: thou knowest that I have affection for thee". He could no longer trust his own estimate of himself, and he referred the whole matter to the One whose estimate he had learned to trust in preference to his own. The sifting and its consequences had done their work. Self-confidence was broken, and replaced by confidence in the Lord.

Then he got his commission, "Feed my lambs ... Shepherd my sheep ... Feed my sheep"; and received a promise that even in death he should glorify God. And as the gospel record closes, on that very shore where first he heard the words, "Follow me", three years and a half before, he hears again from the lips of the risen Lord, "Follow me"; and yet again with increased and personal emphasis, "*Follow thou me*". May that parting word come home to all our hearts with power.

THE PURPOSE AND LOVE OF GOD

John 3:14-16

Some scriptures seem to shine with such a brilliancy of grace that they arrest the attention even of the indifferent reader, delight the soul of the anxious one, and are a joy forever to the believer's heart. Such is the scripture we have read. These verses have been called "The Bible in miniature", and as long as the day of grace continues, and the Spirit of God enables evangelists of Christ to preach the gospel, these will be words whereby men shall be saved.

I wish to speak briefly of three things which are here presented very distinctly. (1) The *purpose* of God for man's blessing; (2) the great *necessity* which came across the divine purpose and had to be met before that purpose could be carried out; and (3) the love which was behind all -- which formed the purpose and met the necessity.

God has formed a purpose to have men in infinite blessing before Him. It is His purpose and pleasure that whosoever believes on His Son "should not perish, but have everlasting life". Everything under the sun is of a perishable order. Death is stamped upon everything in the world, and on man himself. But it is God's pleasure to make Himself known to men in the blessedness of His nature, and thus to bring them into the knowledge and joy of that which lies altogether outside the power of death. If our hearts find their object and their joy in things under the sun, we shall prove in the end, like Solomon, that all is vanity. The things will perish from us, or we shall perish from them; all will end in perdition and death. God is not in these things, and death must come in on all the things in which God is not. But by sending His Son into the world God has placed the knowledge of Himself within the reach of men, and this in pure grace and blessing. God has given His only begotten Son; He has not come as a creditor to claim what was due to Him, but as a giving God. All that God is in the blessedness of His nature is set forth in His Son, and all is brought near to men as a gift. Philosophers of many ages have spent long and fruitless years in the endeavour by searching to find out God. Religious men have sought to remove the distance between themselves and God by prayers, penances, and innumerable ceremonies and sacraments. But the thought that God should present Himself in all His infinite perfections to men, and that all should be a GIFT, confounds the human mind, while it is an endless joy and wonder to faith.

As the Son of God becomes our object and joy we pass outside the range of death. Death cannot touch or mar the blessedness of that which is set forth in Him. The revelation of God that subsists in Him is perfect and eternal, and in entering into it we enter into that which in its very nature is imperishable and eternal. We have everlasting life. And this is the great blessing which God has purposed for man. In the accomplishment of this great result divine love finds its satisfaction and rest.

But between this blessed purpose of God and its accomplishment there came in a great divine necessity occasioned by the sinful state of men. Men were fallen, and lost, and under death and judgment. All this had to be taken into account. God's purpose for man's blessing could only be carried out on the ground that God undertook the settlement of every question in connection with man's sinful state. Hence the "must ... be" of John 3:14.

"And as Moses lifted up the serpent in the wilderness, even so must the Son of man be lifted up". He who "came down from heaven", and ever was even here "in heaven" as the home and atmosphere to which His moral perfections properly belonged, must be "lifted up". God made the Son of man strong for Himself (Psalm 80:17) -- strong to come into the place of sin, and to discharge in death the penalties which were the consequence of sin -- strong to bring to an end in holy judgment the very state of man to which sin attached.

The serpent of Moses had no poison in it, but it was made like the creatures who had, and so

God has sent His own Son -- holy, undefiled, and without sin -- in the likeness of sinful flesh. That Holy One has been "lifted up" as a sacrifice for sin, and thus sin in the flesh has been condemned (Romans 8:3). He "must" be lifted up! The universe must know that God is "glorious in holiness" -- that He will maintain His own righteousness, and vindicate at His own cost every attribute of His Being, while He acts according to His blessed nature that He may accomplish the purposes of His love.

Thus, God stands revealed. It is not only blessings that are presented, but all the blessedness of God Himself. "He is in the light". No clouds and thick darkness round about Him now. His attributes are fully displayed, in all their perfection; His nature has disclosed itself. "GOD IS LOVE". To know Him, and Jesus Christ His sent One, is life eternal.

DECISION FOR CHRIST

I would not speak of decision for Christ to a careless sinner who had neither felt the burden of his sins nor believed in the Lord Jesus. Harm is often done by calling upon ungodly sinners to decide for Christ, and perhaps to stand up in token that they have done so. The effect is to occupy them with some act of their own, rather than with Christ and the grace of God. They feel *they* have done something, and this is very injurious to them spiritually, even when there is a real work of God in them. Alas! many have "decided for Christ" just as they might have taken a temperance pledge, without any sense of their lost condition, or any real work of God's Spirit in their souls.

But there are many souls who have been truly convicted of sin, and whose hearts have turned to the Lord Jesus as their Saviour, who have not had courage to confess His name; they have not come to the point of definitely taking a stand for Christ. It is with this class in view that I desire to say a few words on decision for Christ.

In connection with this I may say that Satan always does his best to hinder souls from taking the next step.

This is true from the beginning to the end of

the soul's history. God takes us up in His grace and leads us on step by step, and whatever may be the next step that God would have us take is just the very point at which all Satan's forces will be concentrated to hinder us. For instance, when one begins to be troubled about his sins Satan will bring in a hundred things to stop the exercise. Friends will be more entertaining than ever, one's attention will be diverted perhaps to politics, to some form of pleasure one never thought of before, to some interesting book, to some hobby or other, to some religious work, to some scheme for doing good; anything and everything will be brought in to diminish or destroy that exercise of conscience before God which is making the soul feel its deep need of salvation.

But if soul-concern cannot be dismissed by these means - and, thank God, it cannot when His Spirit is at work - if in spite of all this the sense of need continues and the distress of soul deepens, Satan falls back a step and rallies all his hosts at another point. He does all he can now to darken the gospel by turning souls in upon themselves - their works, prayers, experience, feelings, repentance, faith, etc., etc. Whole regiments of doubts, fears, questionings, and misapprehensions confront the anxious one to hinder him from looking only and altogether to Christ.

But grace triumphs in the end, and the believer looks away from himself to Jesus. He finds the whole foundation of his confidence in Another. He sees that God has provided a Saviour worthy of all his trust. He accepts for himself the faithful saying that Christ Jesus came into the world to save sinners. He believes on God who raised that blessed One from the dead, and, having righteousness imputed to him, and being justified by faith, he enters into peace with God through the Lord Jesus Christ.

Now he is ready for a third step, and the warfare wages round another movement. It is at this point the question of decision for Christ comes plainly to the front. Now Satan's object will be to hinder him from confessing Christ. He will heap all kinds of real or imaginary difficulties in the way of taking a stand for the Lord. He will make it apparently the most difficult thing in the world to come out simply and decidedly for Christ. He knows well how to work on the timidity of the flesh, and to use the fear of man to ensnare the soul. The pride of the flesh is also a great hindrance. We are often so painfully sensitive as to what people may say or think of us - so terribly unwilling to make fools of ourselves in the eyes of our worldly friends. And in some cases souls are hindered by the pious fear that they might break down and dishonour the worthy Name.

Now let me seek to encourage you to take the decisive step. In the first place, I am sure that you would be happier. You are ill at ease in your present position, for it is in one way a false one. You are like a man who has joined the army and taken the shilling, but has not yet put on the regimentals. Your very indecision leads you into trouble, for you get into conversation with the ungodly, and are carried on from one thing to another until, like Lot, your soul is vexed with the filthy conversation and unlawful deeds of the wicked, and you have no power to resist it or to escape from it, because you are ashamed to avow that you belong to the Lord Jesus. If you took a distinct stand you would escape from very much of this.

And further, you would be supported by the power of God. A believer who does not take a stand for the Lord does not get divine support. If I went to some foreign country and by carefully concealing the fact that I was an Englishman, led everybody to conclude that I was a native of that foreign country, I could not complain if, when troubles arose, the British Government did not interfere on my behalf. In such a case they might justly say, "We will support with all our power the honour of the British flag, but we will not support a man who is ashamed of that flag". All the power of God will support the honour of the Name of the Lord Jesus. Divine support, and security for the believer against all the power of evil, are connected with the fact that he confesses the Lord Jesus. He has come under a lordship of blessing and gracious power of which he is not ashamed. And he gets the support of that power by the Spirit to maintain him against all the power of evil here. Rahab "bound the scarlet line in the window" (Joshua 2), and thus put herself under the protection of Jehovah. It was the confession that she submitted to His righteousness, and put her trust in His grace and power. She connected herself thus with His Name, and He became her security against every evil.

Shadrach, Meshach, and Abed-nego present a fine example of whole-hearted decision. "O Nebuchadnezzar, we are not careful to answer thee in this matter. If it be so, our God, whom we serve, is able to deliver us from the burning fiery furnace; and he will deliver us out of thine hand, O king. But if not, be it known unto thee, O king, that we will not serve thy gods, nor worship the golden image which thou hast set up" (Daniel 3:16-18). Believers are often exceedingly "careful" not to involve themselves in any suffering or loss for Christ, but by such a course they deprive themselves of the true power and joy of Christianity, and of much honour that God would put upon them. They need to drink a little more into the spirit of the apostles, who rejoiced "that they were counted worthy to suffer shame for his name" (Acts 5:41).

Moses refused greatness in Egypt, even when it had been put within his reach by the providence of God. He chose "to suffer affliction with the people of God". It was not that he submitted to it as an unavoidable trial. He voluntarily chose it, "esteeming the reproach of Christ greater riches than the treasures in Egypt: for he had respect unto the recompense of the reward" (Hebrews 11:24-26). This is the course that faith takes. It throws in its lot with the despised and suffering "people of God", and esteems itself a gainer by having exchanged the good things of this life and the pleasures of sin for "the reproach of Christ" and "the sufferings of this present time".

I wish now to bring before you another aspect of decision for Christ, of which we find an illustration in Genesis 24. "And the servant brought forth jewels of silver, and jewels of gold, and raiment, and gave them to Rebecca: he gave also to her brother and to her mother precious things. And they did eat and drink, he and the men that were with him, and tarried all night; and they rose up in the morning, and he said, Send me away unto my master. And her brother and her mother said, Let the damsel abide with us a few days, at the least ten; after that she shall go. And he said unto them, Hinder me not, seeing the Lord hath prospered my way; send me away that I may go to my master. And they said, We will call the damsel and enquire at her mouth. And they called Rebecca, and said unto her, Wilt thou go with this man? And she said, I will go" (verses 53-58).

Abraham's steward had come to Mesopotamia

to secure a bride for Isaac, and his mission presents an undoubted type of the present activity of the Spirit of God who has come down from a glorified Christ to secure hearts for Him. I am not speaking of His activity towards sinners now, but of His work in saints. He has come to secure the bridal affections of the church for Christ. The first part of His service in view of this is to give us conscious suitability for Christ. "The servant brought forth jewels of silver, and jewels of gold, and raiment, and gave them to Rebecca". All these things came from Abraham's house, from the place where Isaac was; they formed no part of Rebecca's possessions as the daughter of Bethuel. Everything was conferred upon her from Isaac's side so that she might be altogether suitable for him.

According to new creation we derive everything from Christ. We are not brought to Him in imperfection and nakedness, but as those who derive all from Him, and have everything in Him, and are "all of one" with Him. The knowledge of this sets our hearts free to be entirely for Him. It is the service of the Spirit to make this good in our hearts.

But there is sure to be opposition to the Spirit's work in this direction. As in Rebecca's case, "her brother and her mother said, Let the damsel abide with us a few days, at the least ten; after that she shall go"; so in our case every natural and worldly influence will tend to delay the decision of the affections for Christ. Yea, the enemy will use the best things of earth to diminish in our hearts the present attractiveness of heaven and the One who is there. The knowledge of forgiveness, and the certainty of heaven by-and-by, may be possessed without the heart being wholly secured in bridal affection for Christ in glory. Yet it is the Spirit's blessed mission to conduct us now to Him, and a truly decided and devoted heart would refuse to be diverted from Him, or delayed in the moral journey that leads to Him.

It is possible to learn the whole system of Christian doctrine, to be faithful and consistent in one's pathway, to teach, distribute tracts, and preach the gospel, and yet fail to respond to the present mission of the Spirit of God.

"Wilt thou go with this man?" is a blessed and yet searching question which is being raised as distinctly today with the saints of God as it was with Rebecca. It is a question with every one of us here, whether we are content to settle down with the assurance of divine grace and blessing, and into a regular kind of religious life on earth, or whether we respond with whole-hearted affection to the Spirit whose mission it is to conduct us now to Christ in glory.

The Spirit is not an influence which controls us in an indefinite way. He is a divine Person who has a definite mission to lead us outside everything here to Christ. The question, "Wilt thou go with this man?" is thus a very present and practical test for our hearts. We are called upon to decide whether self, the world, service, etc., are to be the present goal for our hearts, or Christ. Rebecca was prepared to leave everything to go to the one who was on the other side of the desert. Are we prepared to say, as she did, "I will go"?

There is no lack of power to carry us thus in spirit to the One who is the Son of the Father's love if we have affection and decision of heart to go. The Spirit's power waits upon us to carry us along in that moral journey to which His own blessed ministry of Christ has incited us. Rebecca "rode upon the camels, and followed the man". Not only did she speak with her lips, but her whole course of life was at once changed, and became the witness to her heart's decision. Many are found to express a certain amount of *desire* after Christ which has little practical result. There must be *decision* of heart which makes us willing to be carried by the Spirit's power away from our own things. We cannot cling in our hearts to things here without being detained from pressing on after Christ.

In Philippians 3, we find a man wholly decided for Christ. Many things had been gain to him as a religious man on earth, but he counted them "loss for Christ". Yea, he counted all things but loss for the excellency of the knowledge of

Christ Jesus his Lord. The Spirit's power was carrying him along in a course of which Christ in glory was the goal. And he not only had the Spirit's object before him, but he was seeking to reach that object by the Spirit's way. Of the servant in Genesis 24 it is said that he "took Rebecca and went his way". Many fail to reach Christ because they do not *follow the man* - they do not go the Spirit's way. They are busy in the endeavour to reach Christ by way of religious flesh. Nothing attracts them unless they can attach it to themselves as men and women in the flesh. If they can be more earnest or useful in service, or more holy in life, they find satisfaction in it, without always detecting that this is still self. It may be pious self, but pious self is not Christ.

The Spirit's way is by the cross. He leads the soul into the recognition of what has been effected by the cross of Christ. Man in the flesh is under death. He may be wise, prudent, mighty, noble, or pious, but he is under death. The cross is the witness of this. Man in the flesh has no place with God; he has been removed in holy judgment in the death of Christ: The Spirit leads us by this road. He brings the cross experimentally into our souls, and thus puts us into accord with the mind of God. That is, the one who travels by the Spirit's way is brought to say experimentally, "I am crucified with Christ" (Galatians 2:20).

The Spirit can only lead in one direction. Man

in the flesh is of no account with Him, and Christ is everything. If we follow, we shall find ourselves carried away from all that we are, as being caused to realise its utter worthlessness before God and rejection by Him. But we shall be brought into the blessed apprehension of Christ, and made to know Him as the gain of our hearts. We shall be moved morally away from that which is defective at every point, and we shall acquire perfection in having Christ for our gain. Thus our hearts, in growing acquaintance with His deep perfections, will be formed in bridal affection and in moral correspondence with Himself.

Once more I ask in closing, Are we prepared to say, "I will go"? May God by His Spirit graciously give us all more decision for Christ.

THE TEACHING OF GRACE

Titus 2:11-14

Grace not only brings salvation, but it teaches us how to live "in this present world". The law was a perfect standard for man upon earth, but it had no power to bring men into conformity with its demands. But grace, acting through the divine nature by the Spirit, brings those who are under its teaching into moral suitability to God. It does not merely impose from without a rule of conduct or a code of morals. It produces new tastes and moral sensibilities in the soul of the believer. In short, it gives God a place in our hearts, and this puts an entirely new complexion upon everything.

"This present world" is characterised by *ungodliness*. Men make their plans, decide their course and order all their way without any reference to God. He is not in all their thoughts. They may have a "form of godliness", but it exercises no practical power over them; they deny the power thereof (2 Timothy 3:5). Instead of being regulated by the fear of God, unconverted men are controlled by "worldly lusts". They are lovers of self, of money, and of pleasure.

The believer who has come under grace has turned his back upon all this. He has denied "ungodliness and worldly lusts". He counts that the time past of his life may suffice him to have wrought the will of the Gentiles. He now arms himself with the mind to suffer in the flesh, knowing that "he that hath suffered in the flesh hath ceased from sin; that he no longer should live the rest of his time in the flesh to the lusts of men, but to the will of God" (1 Peter 4:1-3). He yields himself unto God, and his members as instruments of righteousness unto God (Romans 6:13). He takes a decided stand against sin and the lusts of the flesh.

Then, as having taken this stand, grace teaches us to "live soberly, righteously, and godly in this present world". Naturally we are all, more or less, inflated with self-importance; we entertain an exaggerated opinion of ourselves. Sobriety is the contrast to this. Grace teaches true modesty and moderation of mind; it gives us a proper estimate of ourselves, so that we do not think more highly of ourselves than we ought to think (Romans 12:3). If we are taught by grace we shall not have very large thoughts of ourselves. If Paul was "less than the least of all saints", what size are we?

The teaching of grace sets aside in our spirits the self-importance of nature, and thus delivers us from many sorrows. Nine-tenths of the troubles, heart-burnings, and personal jars which disturb and distress the children of God arise from a self-importance which is easily offended, and are kept alive by a self-importance which will not take a low place and confess its ungracious acts and words. If we lack the grace of God and its blessed teaching, we need not be surprised to find roots of bitterness springing up to trouble and defile us.

Then grace teaches us to live "righteously". I should not think much of a professed convert who did not desire to pay his debts and to make reparation for any injury he might have done in his unconverted days. A young man who had been for years robbing his employers was recently converted. One of the first things he did after his conversion was to confess the whole thing, and to beg that he might be allowed to remain with his salary reduced by half until the amount stolen should be refunded. His employers, themselves Christians, were greatly touched by this practical outcome of the teaching of grace.

But to live "righteously" includes much more than the obligation to pay debts and make reparation for injuries done. It necessitates that we conduct ourselves toward others in consistency with the grace which has been shown to us. The servant in the parable of Matthew 18:23-25 was wicked because his behaviour to his fellow servant was entirely contrary to the grace which had been shown to himself. It is *unrighteous* for the Christian to be hard and exacting with others when such infinite *grace* has been shown to himself. God's idea of a "just [righteous]" man includes the thought of mercy and consideration for others (see Matthew 1:19). We find this also in the Old Testament. "The righteous sheweth mercy and giveth" (Psalm 37:21). Indeed, the righteous man is the one who acts on the same principles as God. Psalm 111 and Psalm 112 are very interesting and instructive in this connection. Psalm 111 is descriptive of Jehovah, and Psalm 112 of the man that fears Jehovah. A comparison of the two psalms will show that what is said of Jehovah in one is said of the man that fears Him in the other. So in the New Testament saints are viewed as having "put on the new man, which *after God* is created in righteousness and true holiness" (Ephesians 4:24).

Grace teaches us to behave "as becometh the gospel of Christ" (Philippians 1:27), and to "walk worthy of God" (1 Thessalonians 2:12). We thus become the practical exponents of God's character in a world where He is unknown, and show forth the excellencies of Him who has called us out of darkness into His marvellous light (1 Peter 2:9).

As taught by grace, the believer lives "soberly, righteously, and godly, in this present world". He dreads the self-will and independence of spirit which shuts God out of the hearts of men. He loves to walk in lowliness and piety as one who trusts in the living God. Prayer becomes a constant necessity to him. He walks before

God and acknowledges God in all his ways.

How blessed to be thus formed by the teaching of grace in moral suitability to God! May each believer on the Lord Jesus Christ be found living "soberly, righteously, and godly, in this present world; looking for that blessed hope, and the glorious appearing of the great God and our Saviour Jesus Christ; who gave himself for us, that he might redeem us from all iniquity, and purify unto himself a peculiar people, zealous of good works!"

A SONG OF THE BELOVED

Psalm 45

This is a psalm for those who love the Lord. It is, as the title expresses it, "A song of the Beloved". If you do not *love* the Lord Jesus you will not enjoy or even understand it. All true believers love the Lord Jesus. When Paul by the Holy Spirit said at the end of his letter to the Ephesians, "Grace be with all them that *love* our Lord Jesus Christ in sincerity", he invoked a blessing upon every true Christian. When the same apostle wrote to the Corinthians he had to rebuke them sharply for bad doctrines and bad practices, but there is nothing like a curse in it until the very end. When Paul took the pen to sign the letter he added these solemn words, "If any man *love* not the Lord Jesus Christ, let him be Anathema Maranatha" - accursed before the Lord at His coming. Christianity is a vast cluster of spiritual blessings, but the brighter the light, the deeper is the shadow which it casts. This is what I may call the shadow cast by the light of grace when it is hindered from shining on the soul by enmity and unbelief of heart. God forbid that the dark shadow of that awful curse should ever fall upon your spirit!

Believers love the Lord Jesus for two great reasons because of what He has done for them, and because of what He is in Himself. I am addressing you as those who know, through grace, in some measure what the Lord has done for you. This is a psalm for the sons of Korah; and what the Lord did for them is a very striking picture of what He has done for us.

Read Numbers 16:23-33. The sin of Korah was that he presumed to come near to God in a priestly way without any priestly fitness. To constitute a man a priest he must be chosen and called of God, and have divine title and priestly fitness to approach. Cain was the first to deny this. He presumed to come to God in his own way - in self-will and sin, instead of in the obedience of faith. Korah did the same. Hence Cain and Korah are linked together, with Balaam between them, as solemn warnings to the latter-day apostates of whom Jude writes. Korah shows us the terminus of "the way of Cain"; it leads to the pit. In plain words, the *religion* of man in the flesh is more offensive to God than his *sins*; in fact, it is but the addition of hypocrisy and presumption to his other sins, and it ends in "the pit". So we find this guilty family doomed to destruction, and if we had only Numbers 16, we should conclude that all perished to be witnesses to the severity of the righteous judgment of God. But, blessed be God, His mercy has always rejoiced against judgment, and at the very moment of this appalling act of judgment He secured a marvellous triumph of mercy, and proved for ever that His sovereign grace, which Korah had so despised, would secure blessing for Korah's sons. It is told us in Numbers 26:11, "Notwithstanding the children of Korah died not". When the pit opened her mouth to engulf the presumptuous family, the hand of God was outstretched to snatch the sons of Korah as brands from the burning. They were rescued from the very jaws of hell by the hand of divine grace. Jehovah thus became their Saviour God, and afterwards entrusted them with the charge of the gates of His sanctuary. As belonging to the family which had been doomed to perish for presuming to draw near to God without priestly title, they were the very ones best fitted when saved by sovereign grace, to see that no person approached God but such as had a proper title to stand in His presence. No wonder that the eleven psalms for the sons of Korah are among the sweetest in the book. People saved after such a fashion might well sing sweetly the praises of grace divine; they might well love the Lord for the great work which He had wrought for them.

Christian! behold in their salvation a picture of your own: you were a child in a doomed family, guilty of sins which called loudly for the judgment of God, and the whole course of your unconverted life was a sharp descent to the pit. There was neither eye to pity nor arm to save you until God laid help upon One who was mighty, and found a ransom in the Person of His beloved Son, that you might be delivered from going down to the pit. The hand of mercy arrested you; the Christ of God became all your salvation. And though you have not seen Him, yet, knowing Him by faith, you love Him, and His praise is really to your heart "a Song of the Beloved".

But this is not all. *Love* must have a Person for its object, and always thinks more of the giver than of the gift. *Love* values the benefits it receives not by their intrinsic worth, but by the affections of which they are the expression. The sinner when first awakened to a sense of his danger can rarely think of anything but his own need. And as a rule the first feeling of the soul that trusts the Lord Jesus for salvation is rather one of *gratitude* than of *love*. It is when our need has been met, and our hearts are quite assured as to the benefit, that we begin to learn that love was the source of all our blessing. Behind the work that has been done and the salvation that has been secured there is something greater still, and that is the love which was the source of it all. How this attracts the heart to the Person of the Son of God! He gave Himself for me because He loved me. "Hereby perceive we love, because he laid down his life for us" (1 John 3:16). Faith in Christ is not like the faith that people have in a bank or in a skilled physician; it is faith in *One who has won our hearts*. Hence the *believer* is also a *lover*. "We love him because he first loved us".

It is thus that we are drawn to Christ. He becomes to us "the Beloved", and as our affections go out to Him His moral beauties become the food of our hearts. We delight in Him as the One "fairer than the children of men". Every moral perfection shone out in that blessed One. Whatsoever things are true, honest, just, pure, lovely, and of good report were found in Him. The exhortation to "think on these things" (Philippians 4:8) invites us to contemplate Christ. What a blessed study for the heart! For the One who is thus "fair to God" is *the One who loves us*, and has given Himself for us. The great lack with many believers is that they have not in heart reached Christ so as to delight in His perfections. Hence their hearts do not overflow; they are not conscious of being loved by Him.

But if we reach *Christ* we must of necessity reach Him *where He is*. It could be said of Him when here, "Grace is poured into thy lips". There was a fulness of grace in Him to meet every need. To the sinner He could say, "Thy sins are forgiven"; to the leper, "I will, be thou clean"; to the palsied, "Rise up and walk"; to the blind, "Receive thy sight"; to the dead, "Lazarus, come forth". Thus when on earth the all-varied grace of God revealed itself in Him. He was ever the Centre of a circle of blessing; virtue went out of Him to meet every necessity of faith. And it is not less so today. Indeed the lovely pictures which are presented to us in the pages of the evangelists are divinely illustrative of the spiritual needs of our souls and of the perfect answer to all these needs which we may find in Him. But He is now *in another place.* Rejected and put in the place of curse by man, God has blessed Him for ever in another place. God has said to Him, "Sit thou at my right hand, until I make thine enemies thy footstool" (Psalm 110:1). And the only circle of blessing is where Christ is. We come into heavenly blessing by being *associated with Christ in glory.* This is plainly suggested to us by the words, "God, thy God, hath anointed thee with the oil of gladness above thy fellows" (verse 7).

Christ in glory has "fellows", but it is impossible for us to understand this if we do not see something of the blessed truth of new creation. As in the flesh it is impossible that we could be "fellows" of Christ. According to the old creation we are "fellows" of the man driven out of Eden as rejected by God. But in new creation we are companions of Christ. "If any man be in Christ there is new creation: old things are passed away; behold, all things are become new. And all things are of God" (2 Corinthians 5:17). Everything in us that is not "of God" was ended in the death of Christ. It was then that the "old things" passed away. The death of Christ is the way by which divine love could bring us into suitability to itself. God "made him to be sin for us, who knew no sin; that we might become the righteousness of God in him" (2 Corinthians 5:21). The death of Christ has pronounced the solemn sentence on Adam's race - "all dead" (2 Corinthians 5:14). Man after the flesh is utterly rejected by God.

But there is new creation, and those "in Christ" are sanctified by His death, they are apart by that death from all that they were as in the flesh, and in new creation they are "all of one" with Christ, and made "accepted in the beloved" (Ephesians 1:6). It is evident that for the enjoyment of this there must be the *appropriation* of the death of Christ; we must eat His flesh and drink His blood. By the appropriation of His death we are severed in heart and spirit from all that we were as in Adam, so that we may be, by the Spirit, in association with Christ as His "fellows". Thus we stand consciously in the place of acceptance - "in gold of Ophir" (Psalm 45:9). In Christ we are in perfect suitability to divine love, and thus free in heart to enter into that love.

The effect of all this is to produce *intense separation of heart* from every association that is of the world or of the earth. This is brought before us in a striking way in Psalm 45:10, "Hearken, O daughter, and consider, and incline thine ear; forget also thine own people, and thy father's house". *Separation* is the natural outcome of conscious *suitability* to

Christ. I am sure that if our hearts were conscious of being in divine suitability to Christ in glory it would make us feel perfect strangers here, and it would break the power of every old association.

We may see in Genesis 24 a picture of how the Spirit of God would detach our hearts from old associations: "And the servant brought forth jewels of silver and jewels of gold, and raiment, and gave them to Rebekah" (verse 53). No doubt the jewels and the raiment came from Abraham's house - from the place where Isaac was; and invested with that which came *from him*, she was made consciously suitable *for him*. This is how the Spirit would work. He would invest us with conscious suitability *for* Christ because deriving everything from Him. Thus was Rebekah prepared to face the question "Wilt thou go with this man?" and to give the decisive answer, "I will go". It involved breaking with her own people and her father's house, and a journey of perhaps 500 miles across the desert, but she was prepared for all this. The attractions of Isaac had eclipsed everything else for her heart, and she was free in affection to go to him because conscious of suitability for him. Beloved brethren, are we prepared to take the moral journey of which hers was such a striking type? The Spirit of God is here to conduct us to Christ where He is. I do not mean when we die or when He comes. The Spirit would lead our hearts to Him now. But this involves a moral journey; it involves heart-separation from things and associations here.

And in Psalm 45: 10, this is connected with *hearkening* and *considering.* Clean animals (Leviticus 11) *chew the cud* and *part the hoof.* To hearken and consider answers to chewing the cud, and forgetting our own people and our father's house is like parting the hoof. If there was more *meditation,* I feel sure there would be more *separation.* If we digested the communications of divine love into our moral being, they would necessarily lead to separation. Mary, in Luke 10, is hearkening and considering; in John 12, she forgets her own people and her father's house - the poor in Israel. She was entirely separated in heart to Christ, and there was but one to approve her action. She was exclusively for Christ. She had found satisfaction in Him, and she was separated to Him.

I think you will find these two thoughts continually presented together in Scripture. If we hear the voice of the Shepherd we shall follow Him, and in following *Him* we shall be drawn apart from everything that is not *Him.* If our hearts feed on that which is of God, we shall be kept at a moral distance from that which is of man. Jeremiah could say, "Thy words were found, and I did eat them; and thy word was unto me the joy and rejoicing of mine heart"; but the effect of this was that he also said, "I sat not in the assembly of the mockers, nor rejoiced; I sat alone" (Jeremiah 15:16,17). The blessed man of Psalm 1 delights in the law of Jehovah, and meditates therein day and night; and, on the other hand, he neither walks in the counsel of the ungodly, nor stands in the way of sinners, nor sits in the seat of the scornful. He chews the cud and parts the hoof.

It is only the satisfied heart that can be truly a separated heart. I am sure that *inward* separation is the great thing, and it is of special importance in a day when the principle of outward separation from glaring evils is so widely accepted. Lot was outwardly separate when he was with Abraham, but he was not inwardly separate. His heart hankered after such things as he had seen in Egypt, and as soon as opportunity offered he forsook the path of separation altogether. Swine are unclean because they part the hoof without chewing the cud. They are typical of those who, like the Pharisees, are outwardly separate without any inward assimilation of the mind of God.

"So shall the king greatly desire thy beauty" (Psalm 45:11). How suggestive is this to our hearts of the fact that the church is the object of *the love of Christ*! He "loved the church, and gave himself for it; that he might sanctify and cleanse it with the washing of water by the word, that he might present it to himself a glorious church, not having spot, or wrinkle, or any such thing; but that it should be holy and without blemish" (Ephesians 5:25-27). The present satisfaction of the heart of Christ is found in having the church altogether for Himself. To this end He gave Himself for it; He "sold all that he had, and bought" the "pearl of great price"; and to this end He sanctifies and cleanses it with the washing of water by the word. By giving Himself for it He secured the right to have the church in eternal suitability to His own love, and now He sanctifies and cleanses it so as to bring it into present moral suitability to Himself. His love is active to remove every blemish - every spot and wrinkle. He desires to present the church to Himself *even now* in the moral glory and beauty of complete sanctification from everything that is not of Himself.

It may be asserted that the church does not answer to this, and that to speak of it is to set up an impracticable ideal. I am sure that if there is true affection for Christ in our hearts we shall not think that His thoughts are impracticable, or that He is incapable of making them good for our souls. We may have to confess that we have very feebly answered to His thoughts, and that we have oftentimes hindered Him from sanctifying and cleansing us, but by His grace we cleave to Him, and we treasure in our souls the precious thoughts of His love which passeth knowledge. That there is but little answer to those thoughts in the church must be sorrowfully owned, but I cannot believe that general decline and departure from first love would have the effect of causing faithful and devoted hearts to be content with something less than what is in the heart of Christ for the church. I think every loyal and loving heart would rather desire to render increasingly to Him the satisfaction for which He looks in vain in those who know not the thoughts of His love.

We must connect the words, “So shall the king greatly desire thy beauty” with the preceding verse. It is as we are in true separation to Himself that we minister to the satisfaction of His heart. The church’s beauty in the eyes of Christ is her sanctification. There is a day coming when she will be “as a bride adorned for her husband”, and it is a pity if we do not long to be morally adorned for Him now. If you read John 13-John 17, you will find how every desire of the heart of Christ wraps itself round His own which are in the world. We may learn there what we are to Him and how He would have us adorned for Him. The more we enter into what the church is according to the thoughts of divine love, the better we shall understand her attractiveness and beauty in the eyes of Christ. Her beauty is moral correspondence to Himself. May each of us covet to be invested with more of this “beauty of holiness”!

“The king’s daughter is all glorious within; her clothing is of wrought gold; she shall be brought unto the king in raiment of needlework" (Psalm 45:13, 14). It is "within" the ivory palaces - "within" the royal courts - that the King's daughter is "all glorious". The beauty of the saints does not yet appear in public view. *Without* they may be despised as an ignorant and cursed rabble (John 7:49), they may be reviled and cast out (John 9:28, 34; John 12:42), but *within* His pavilion, and in the secret of His tabernacle, they are "all glorious" as loved by the Father and the Son and indwelt by the Comforter. The glory of the church is hidden from the pride of man in the secret of His presence. But it will not be ever thus. "When Christ, who is our life, shall appear, then shall ye also appear with him in glory" (Colossians 3:4). The glorious beauty of the church will be manifested; she will appear in clothing of "wrought gold". How fair the scene that lies before us! The saints in new creation beauty, and made the righteousness of God in Christ, will be displayed in a perfection that is wholly of God. "The glory which thou gavest me I have given them; that they may be one, even as we are one; I in them, and thou in me, that they may be made perfect in one; and that the world may know that thou hast sent me, and hast loved them as thou hast loved me" (John 17:22, 23).

And let us not forget the "raiment of needlework". It is blessed to know that in every one who has received the Spirit there must have been produced some of His precious fruit. The "righteousnesses of the saints" (Revelation 19:8) can only be those things which have been wrought in us by the Spirit. Blessed be God! none of His fruit can ever perish. Nothing that is according to God's will in the saints will ever be lost. No action, or word, or thought that was pleasing to God will be overlooked in that day when the Lord will both "bring to light the hidden things of darkness, and will make manifest the counsels of the hearts: and then shall every man have praise of God" (1 Corinthians 4:5).

To the Lamb's wife will be "granted that she should be arrayed in fine linen, clean and white: for the fine linen is the righteousnesses of the saints". She will be invested for ever with raiment which was wrought stitch by stitch in practical loyalty to Christ and to the blessed will of God here in this world. The bride is making her wedding-dress *now*. I trust that, constrained by the love of Christ, we may increasingly live unto Him.

---

www.ingramcontent.com/pod-product-compliance
Lightning Source LLC
LaVergne TN
LVHW050635100826
845148LV00011B/1869

* 9 7 8 0 9 1 2 8 6 8 3 0 1 *